"I love the Book of Proverbs. It weaves deep theology with the kind of practical handles a guy like me needs every single day. That's also why I love *Choose Wisely, Live Fully*. Donna Gaines does a great job balancing the unvarnished truth of Scripture with real-life application. That powerful combination can change your life—and the lives of those you love."

—**Dave Ramsey**, best-selling author and nationally syndicated radio show host

"Donna Gaines writes in a way that allows the reader to absorb profound truth deep into the heart, mind, and soul. She is a modern-day Deborah, declaring the Scriptures as the ultimate source of wisdom for every woman who dares to choose a life of no regrets. You will come away from these pages with full confidence in the love and sovereignty of God."

—**Diane Strack**, speaker, teacher, co-founder of Student Leadership University, and author of *New Start for Single Moms*, *Quiet Influence*, and coauthor of *Good Kids Who Do Bad Things*.

"*Choose Wisely, Live Fully* creates a beautiful launching pad from which women can not only learn but also share biblical truths that have the capacity to change their lives and the lives of generations to come. Donna and her daughters share personal stories and godly wisdom that bring the book of Proverbs alive. A teacher at heart, Donna skillfully equips women with practical tools to help those we love choose the path that leads to the abundant life Jesus promises. The path that will fill them with godly confidence, self-worth, purpose, and direction."

—**Wendy Blight**, author and writer for the Proverbs 31 Ministries First 5 app

"The Book of Proverbs is a book of wisdom that I have studied my entire life. Author Donna Gaines takes the lessons of Proverbs and gives anointed, spirit-filled insight on discipleship. *Choose Wisely, Live Fully* is a book that helps us understand the wisdom of Proverbs and how to apply it to our everyday lives. This discipleship tool will challenge you personally and will strengthen you to mentor others to walk in wisdom."

—**Ellen Olford**, Director of Women, Central Church

"Every choice we make has a correlating eternal consequence. In her powerful book, *Choose Wisely, Live Fully*, Donna Gaines challenges us in a fresh way to make wise decisions, choices that glorify God and yield blessings. Using the two women in Proverbs, Wisdom and Folly, she stirs within us a robust desire to walk in absolute obedience to the Word of God. This book is a must read for women who are ready to be stirred and changed; when you reach the last page, you will not be the same."

—**Dayna Street**, Women's Ministry Director, Bellevue Baptist Church

"Donna Gaines is a woman of the Word! In *Choose Wisely, Live Fully*, we are shown how to walk in obedience to the Lord and His Word in a world that is trying to pull us in the opposite direction. Donna offers practical ways on how to pursue a life of holiness and guides us in how to make wise choices in our everyday life. I look forward to using this book as a resource with discipleship groups in the future."

—**Kandi Gallaty**, coauthor of *Foundations*

"*Choose Wisely, Live Fully* by Donna Gaines is an eye-opening window to Proverbs for today's generation. Donna's teaching, inspired through the Holy Spirit, is simply stated yet life-changing. I personally have read through the Book of Proverbs more times than I can count, however, Donna's insights have given me a brand-new perspective with applications I had never considered. She has a gift of bringing truths to a new light, and that light points straight to our Creator."

—**Shari Falwell**

CHOOSE WISELY, LIVE FULLY

LESSONS FROM WISDOM & FOLLY,
THE TWO WOMEN OF PROVERBS

DONNA GAINES

ABINGDON PRESS
NASHVILLE

CHOOSE WISELY, LIVE FULLY
LESSONS FROM THE BOOK OF PROVERBS

Copyright © 2017 by Donna Dodds Gaines

Library of Congress Cataloging-in-Publication Data has been requested.
ISBN 978-1-5018-3424-0

Unless otherwise indicated, all Scripture quotations are taken from the New American Standard Bible® (NASB), Copyright © 1960, 1962, 1963, 1968, 1971, 1972, 1973, 1975, 1977, 1995 by The Lockman Foundation. Used by permission. www.Lockman.org

Scripture quotations marked ICB are taken from the International Children's Bible®. Copyright © 1986, 1988, 1999 by Thomas Nelson, Inc. Used by permission. All rights reserved.

Scripture quotations marked MSG are taken from THE MESSAGE, copyright © 1993, 1994, 1995, 1996, 2000, 2001, 2002 by Eugene H. Peterson. Used by permission of NavPress. All rights reserved. Represented by Tyndale House Publishers, Inc.

Scripture quotations marked (NLT) are taken from the Holy Bible, New Living Translation, copyright © 1996, 2004, 2015 by Tyndale House Foundation. Used by permission of Tyndale House Publishers, Inc., Carol Stream, Illinois 60188. All rights reserved.

Scripture quotations marked (NIV) are taken from the Holy Bible, New International Version®, NIV®. Copyright © 1973, 1978, 1984, 2011 by Biblica, Inc.™ Used by permission of Zondervan. All rights reserved worldwide. www.zondervan.com The "NIV" and "New International Version" are trademarks registered in the United States Patent and Trademark Office by Biblica, Inc.™

Scripture quotations marked (The Voice) are taken from The Voice™. Copyright © 2012 by Ecclesia Bible Society. Used by permission. All rights reserved. Note: Italics in quotations from The Voice are used to "indicate words not directly tied to the dynamic translation of the original language" but that "bring out the nuance of the original, assist in completing ideas, and...provide readers with information that would have been obvious to the original audience" (The Voice, preface). Emphasis in quotations from The Voice is indicated with the use of **boldface** type.

17 18 19 20 21 22 23 24 25 26—10 9 8 7 6 5 4 3 2 1

MANUFACTURED IN THE UNITED STATES OF AMERICA

Dedicated to my granddaughters:
Alivia Jean
Ivey Elizabeth
Ruthie Gail
Hadley Anne
Camille Joy
Emery Kate
and any future granddaughters with whom the Lord gifts us.

So, my son [daughter], follow your father's direction,
and don't forget what your **mother taught you**—
Keep their teachings close to your heart;
engrave them on a pendant, *and hang it around your neck.*
Their instruction will guide you along your journey,
guard you when you sleep,
and address you when you wake in the morning.
For their direction is a lamp; their instruction will light *your path,*
and their discipline will correct your missteps,
sending you down the right **path of life**.

—Proverbs 6:20-23 The Voice, emphasis added

Charm is deceitful and beauty is vain,
But a woman who fears the LORD, *she shall be praised.*

—Proverbs 31:30

Contents

PREFACE

Enthralled

I am incredibly blessed to be the mother of four children. Our oldest child is a son, and the other three are daughters. When our oldest daughter was in the ninth grade, our youth pastor started a discipleship program that he called God-Walkers. I taught Sunday school in our youth department but wanted my daughter under other godly women who would reinforce the truths we were teaching at home. So she was in a different class than the one I taught.

When our youth pastor mentioned discipleship, I had a sudden urge to disciple my daughter and her three best friends. I approached her about it, and she was agreeable. We began meeting each Wednesday afternoon before their youth group Bible study, and we met weekly for four years. I later discipled my other daughters and am so thankful for their personal walks with Christ. For those of you who may be reading this book to learn how to mentor or disciple younger women, I encourage you and tell you from experience that the extra effort and expense is more than worth it! We will go into more detail as we move through our study. I have also provided additional resources in the appendices.

I now qualify as the "older" woman mentioned in Titus 2. My three daughters are grown and married, and two of them have daughters of their own. It is incumbent upon me to continue to pass on to the next generation the wise truths the Lord has revealed. It is my mandate from the Lord. It is "our" mandate, since all of us have someone who is not quite as far down the road in age or spiritual maturity as we are.

I write predominantly for women, but the truths contained in this study are for all people. In fact, the Book of Proverbs was written by a king for his children. So if you are the mother of sons, these truths are transferable.

If you are a young woman who desires to be discipled, gather together a group of young women and ask them to journey through this book with you. God desires for you to "know" Him intimately and to discern the truths that enable you to choose "life and blessing" at every turn.

There are some things I did to disciple our girls as well as things I did not do that I wish I had done. I would like to pass this knowledge on to you. All of us are on this journey together, the journey that leads home. And it is imperative that we lead those who follow us down the right path, the path that leads to life.

I have invited my daughters to join me in this project. They will honestly and with authenticity share about the truths that were most meaningful to them and how they are now seeking to pass these truths down to their own daughters. Their contributions will be at the end of each chapter dealing with a character quality of Wisdom.

As we study the truths of Scripture, we will contrast the two women of Proverbs: Wisdom and Folly. The only way to be a wise woman is to know Jesus Christ and to fall passionately in love with Him. Knowing you are His and He is yours leads to the unveiling of wisdom that ushers you into the blessed life.

To be enthralled (to hold spellbound, captivated, delighted) with Jesus opens the door to the passion that makes life worth living. We all know that passion for Christ is caught more than it is taught. These are not just truths to "know," they are truths to live!

Living for the legacy,
Donna Gaines

INTRODUCTION

God is relational and has created us in His image. Even though that image is grossly marred, we still have an awareness that we were created for more than this life has to offer, and we long for what should be. God's story of redemption is woven into all of life—music, movies, literature, and even our fairy tales. We long to be rescued, much like the damsel in distress in the fairy tales of our childhood.

As young girls we were drawn to these stories of heroism and rescue because of that longing for more. The Bible tells us in Ecclesiastes 3:11 that God has set eternity in our hearts. The desire for life as it should be has been firmly planted in each person's soul. We know there is more to life than we are experiencing, and we are constantly searching for "happily ever after."

I believe that is the desire behind the popularity of romance novels and "chick flicks." In fact, romance novels are one of the most popular genres of fiction, and according to Romance Writers of America, the largest percent is purchased by women—84 percent.[1]

Reflect on the fairy tales we are all familiar with: Cinderella, Snow White, Sleeping Beauty, Rapunzel, Beauty and the Beast. What do they all have in common? They all contain a rescued damsel who lives happily ever after with her prince. Some have called this longing a faint memory or imprint from creation, an awareness of being created in the image of God and a longing for life eternal, where there is no sickness and separation.

I was reflecting on these truths when I was asked to speak at a father/daughter banquet at our church. As I prepared, I began to think about what it means to be a real princess—a daughter of the King. As I was considering the virtues of princess life, I remembered one of my favorite fairy tales from childhood—Cinderella. Recalling the transforming story of her life, I suddenly realized that there are a number of spiritual parallels between Cinderella's story and the real life journey to become a daughter of the King of the universe.

In Walt Disney's version, Cinderella lived in a beautiful home with her mother and father, and life was good. But then her mother died, and her father married a woman who had two daughters. Life continued, and although it may not have been all that Cinderella desired, it was acceptable until the untimely death of her father. After his death, the true nature of her stepmother was revealed. Cinderella was banished to a room in the attic and treated like a slave. At the same time, her wicked stepsisters were given beautiful clothes, music lessons, and all the luxuries that money could buy.

In the original Grimm Brothers' fairy tale, Cinderella was a nickname given to her because her face would get smudged with ashes and cinders as she cleaned out the fireplaces in her home. Thus, the cruel daughters of her stepmother tauntingly gave her a new name. Her name had been changed, her once beautiful clothing was now dirty and tattered, and she had been demoted from daughter to slave.

Now consider Adam and Eve in the garden at the beginning of time. Life was good. They lived with their Father, and He would walk with them and talk with them. There was no sin. Consequently, there was no shame, no guilt, and no fear. Can you imagine that? Being able to audibly hear the Father's voice as He walked in the garden with you, with nothing to separate you from His presence?

Rich foliage, bountiful vegetation, and lush fruit trees surrounded them. The menu from the garden was colossal—with one exception—there was one tree in the middle of the garden from which they were not to eat or they would die. Never did they question the Father's protective edict. Never, that is, until the entrance of the wicked serpent into their paradise.

Satan began to whisper his cunning lies to Eve. He questioned God's command with, "Did God say...?" casting doubt on God's Word and its validity. Insinuating that God was holding out on her, the serpent told Eve that God knew if she ate from the tree of the knowledge of good and evil she would become like Him. The whispers continued. With just one bite, she would be in control—the master of her own destiny. She looked at the fruit, and as the lust of her flesh and the greed of her heart consumed her, she ate. She then lured her husband to do the same.

Lust and greed conceived and gave birth to sin, which led to death (James 1:15). Immediately their eyes were opened. Instead of the promised elevated status, they were overcome with grief and demoted to experiencing shame, fear, and guilt. As the true nature of the serpent was exposed, the realization of their eternal state enveloped Eve, and she desperately sought for a covering. The covering was not just for her nakedness but for the sin that had ravaged her soul. She found herself separated from Adam and from God. In a futile attempt to cover their shame, Adam and Eve made loin coverings from fig leaves and attempted to hide from God in the garden.

When God called out to Adam, he admitted that he and Eve had been afraid and were hiding from Him. The Lord confronted their sin, and they began blaming each other and God. The punishment for their sin was death—spiritually and then ultimately physically. They were separated from God and banished from the garden to prevent them from eating from the tree of life and living forever in their sinful condition (Genesis 3:22).

The lies of the serpent were very much like the lies of the wicked step-mother. Believing the lie, Adam and Eve lost their innocence and became enslaved by their sin. Their legacy to all humanity became a sin nature upon which the enemy continues to prey.

The wicked stepmother whispered some of the same lies that the enemy whispers to us. "You are dirty. You are unworthy. You will never measure up. You aren't loved."

When we listen to these lies we make wrong choices, just as Adam and Eve did. What are we longing for? Why are we so vulnerable? All of us long to be sought after, fought for, rescued, and loved. We are looking for our prince. We want life to have a happy ending. We want the heroine to marry the hero and live happily ever after. Our dreams will only be realized when we acknowledge that there is only one Prince who can fulfill the desires of our heart, and His name is *Jesus*.

Have you listened to the lies of the enemy? Have they taken hold of your heart? Your circumstances may seem to confirm the lies. Look at Cinderella's circumstances; they seemed to validate all that her wicked stepmother and stepsisters said. But in her heart Cinderella knew there was more. She knew that someday she would be rescued. One day the lies would be swallowed up by the truth. You know it as well. You know you were created for more.

Hope broke through Cinderella's circumstances when she heard that the king had planned a banquet for the prince, and every girl in the king-dom was invited. The prince would be looking for a wife, and the entire kingdom was abuzz. Cinderella was so excited! Maybe, just maybe, she could meet the prince too. But her hopes were dashed when her wicked stepmother piled on additional chores and then at the last minute her step-sisters tore her dress to shreds.

Weeping and crushed, Cinderella ran outside. But alas, as in all good fairy tales, her fairy godmother arrived. She waved her wand and before you knew it, Cinderella was off to the ball in a beautiful dress and horse-drawn carriage. A way had been made.

My favorite scene in the Disney movie is Cinderella's entrance to the ball. The prince sees her, and when their eyes meet, it is as though there is no one else in the room. They dance until midnight, and then she must flee because the spell will be broken.

Cinderella finds herself back at home. She is dressed once again in her tattered rags, but she is changed. She is changed from the inside out. Her circumstances haven't changed, but she has. She dreams of the prince, and she knows that one day he will come for her. As she dreams, she smiles and sings while she works. There is a gleam in her eye and a spring in her step. So much so that even her wicked stepmother notices the change.

And so it is with anyone who meets the Prince of Peace and allows Him to capture his or her heart. Jesus is "the way" (John 14:6) that we come to the Father and are given eternal life. We will never be the same; and as we long for His arrival, we will begin to change from the inside out. Just as the glass slipper would only fit the true princess, the truths of Christ are only for those who have had their hearts enthralled by His love. His truths are like a new wardrobe "custom-made by the Creator, with his label on it" (Colossians 3:9-10 MSG). As we think on his words, we will begin to replace the lies of the enemy and the world with His truth:

- I am loved and significant.
- I am beautiful, created in the very image of God.
- I am clean, forgiven.
- I am a part of the family of God, a joint heir with Christ.
- I am desired: He delights in me.
- My life has purpose: God has a plan.

Just as Cinderella longed for the prince, he longed for her. Our Prince is longing for the day when the Father tells Him it is time to go and get His bride. At the heart of God's Grand Narrative is a love story. In the Old Testament, Israel is betrothed to Jehovah. In the New Testament it is the church who is His bride (Ephesians 5:25-29).

God's desire from the beginning of time was to have a people for Himself, to live in intimate communion. Every little girl dreams of her wedding day. Likewise, believers long for and dream of the day when our Prince will return on a white horse to rescue us and take us to a wedding celebration that is out of this world!

Revelation 19 paints a beautiful picture of the bride dressed in "linen, bright and clean" (v. 8). Our Prince is coming on a white stallion to wage war on our behalf. And the Father, the Creator has invited everyone to the marriage supper of the Lamb. In Revelation 21, the Holy City, the New Jerusalem is adorned as a bride for her husband. And there we will live with Him forever. Revelation 22:17 says, "The Spirit and the bride say, 'Come.' And let the one who hears say, 'Come.' And let the one who is thirsty come; let the one who wishes take the water of life without cost."

Are you ready? Are you longing and preparing for His return? We can choose to give our heart to the Prince and be enthralled by His love. Once He captures our hearts, He changes us—our identity and our destiny.

Or we can choose to keep our hearts for ourselves and go our own way and be like the two wicked stepsisters who were consumed with themselves, unhappy and unsatisfied. Oh sure, sin satisfies for a season, but it is never enough and always leaves us wanting more. Why? Because choosing sin puts us on the path that leads to death, and the only way off that path is to choose Jesus. We can't will ourselves off or deny ourselves off. Choosing Christ above all leads to obedience, which is the path to life.

Cinderella was no longer defined by her circumstances. She was living for someone and something greater than her current experience. In a far greater way, our inner person is awakened to the love and joy that is awaiting us in Christ. When we fall in love with Jesus and immerse ourselves in His Word, we will begin to choose Him at every turn. We will choose to live every day for *that* day—the day we see Him face-to-face! We will be enthralled with our Prince.

Vocabulary.com states the definition for *enthralled* as: "You are enthralled when filled with delight and wonder at something, to the point where time seems to stand still."[2] When we stand in awe and wonder over the great love of our Savior, our love for self diminishes, and sin loses its grip. We choose Jesus, and thus choose life and blessing not just for ourselves but for our descendants as well.

As Gary Thomas said, "When we yearn for our Creator 'as the deer pants for the water' (Psalm 42:1), when we learn to love the Lord our God with all our heart, soul, mind, and strength (Mark 12:30), holiness will be the by-product of our passion. We cease from sin not simply because we are disciplined, but because we have found something better."[3]

My focus is on my Prince, not my circumstances. I am reading His Word
and preparing for His return. May He find me wise!

CHAPTER 1

Truth

Let us begin. *The worship of the Eternal One,* the one True God, *is the first step toward knowledge.*

Fools, however, do not fear God and *cannot stand wisdom or guidance.*

—Proverbs 1:7 The Voice

Once Cinderella met the prince, her heart was assured of his love, and his love changed everything. So it is with our relationship to Christ. When the Prince of Peace captures our hearts, we know we are loved, and His great love changes our perspective on our life and our purpose. Time seems to stand still, just as it did for Cinderella, and we are enthralled with our Prince!

How do we get to know our Prince? We get to know Him by spending time in His Word. Jesus rebuked the Pharisees because they searched the Scriptures thinking that in them they would find eternal life. But Christ told them it was the Scriptures that pointed to Him (John 5:39).

We must choose to take God at His word and believe that all He says is true. Embracing Him through His Word will lead us to trust and love Him as we are commanded to—with all of our heart, soul, mind, and strength (Mark 12:30). This great love alone satisfies and enables us to live the abundant Christian life.

This abundant life that Jesus said He came to give us (John 10:10) is only available for those who believe. What if I told you there are certain truths in Scripture that will change your life if you will just embrace them? Truths so powerful, truths so intertwined in the warp and woof of all that God has created that they have impacted your life whether you are aware of them or not.

How can I be so sure of myself? Well, for one thing I am a grandmother. I have lived long enough to learn much of what I will share with you through experience. I am also a pastor's wife and a Bible study teacher. I have spent many hours immersing myself in the Word of God looking for answers to life's most often posed questions—answers for myself, for my children, and for all the people our ministry touches.

I have read the Bible from front to back every year for more than twenty-five years. I have studied God's revelations of Himself, of humanity, and of sin. I have observed history and also the lives of those around me. What have I discovered? I have discovered that God's Word is true. He alone is faithful; what He says will come to pass, and we cannot get around the consequences of our behavior.

In John 10 the Jews confronted Jesus and wanted to stone Him for blasphemy because He said He was the Son of God. Jesus responded, "Has it not been written in your Law, 'I SAID, YOU ARE GODS'? If he called them gods to whom the Word of God came (and the Scripture cannot be broken), do you say of Him whom the Father sanctified and sent into the world, 'You are blaspheming,' because I said, 'I am the Son of God'?" (John 10:34-36)

Jesus testified that the Word of God cannot be broken. If God has stated it, it will come to pass. This reality should be impetus enough to cause us to want to study God's Word so we know what He has commanded.

The Bible reveals that the God of the Old Testament is the same as the God of the New Testament. God has not changed, and really neither has humankind. The issues and experiences of the people recorded in the Bible are as current as the front page of our newspapers or the home pages of today's blog sites. So why do we keep repeating the same behaviors even though we can see that no one has been able to sidestep God's laws or the consequences of breaking them?

I am convinced the answer to that question is this: most of us honestly don't know what God has said in the first place. So many Christians only know what other people say about God, which leaves the door wide open to individual interpretation, personal agendas, and propaganda in order to make a point. Biblical illiteracy is rampant. People in the church have been as impacted by media and culture as those outside the church. Many church attendees profess Christ and yet deny Him by their behavior. So what are we to do?

Imagine that the two of us are seated at my kitchen table for a cup of tea. I pour hot water into our cups and immerse a tea bag into each one. If I only dip the tea bag into the water for a brief moment and then hand you your cup, you will be shocked—or at least a little puzzled—that I would expect you to drink a cup of hot water when you have expected tea. You might even try to correct me and tell me that I need to allow the tea to steep. And you would be right.

When a tea bag is immersed and allowed to steep, the flavor and color of the water is changed. The water looks different, smells different, and tastes different. It *is* different! And so will you be different when you immerse yourself in the Word of God. Opening your Bible on Sunday morning or reading a passage in a devotional is not immersion. I am talking about having a plan to read God's Word on a daily basis.

Let's begin by seeking God's wisdom and then applying it to our lives. I want you to join me in a study of Proverbs 1–9. As you read this book I will ask you to step back from your circumstances and honestly reflect upon your life and the choices you have made. As we evaluate and think about our lives in light of God's Word, there will be some adjustments to make.

Recently, I heard a speaker say that about 80 percent of people who attend church do not have values-based conversations in the home. I want to help you change that. As we work through this book, I will be helping you articulate the biblical truths I sought to teach my daughters and now seek to share with women everywhere. These are truths that actually have the capacity to change your life and the lives of your descendants, truths that reveal the remarkable difference in those who have become enthralled with Christ and those who are just professing to have a relationship with

Him. We will be able to see how starkly the Bible contrasts these truths in the lives of two women in the Bible, the two women of Proverbs.

At the end of each chapter you will find a section entitled, "Wisdom's Call." These assignments and questions are designed for personal reflection, but they are also appropriate for sharing in the context of a small group. We are much more likely to follow through on the commitments the Lord is calling us to when we have accountability. The Lord has created us for relationship, and this connection to others will enhance your spiritual growth. If you haven't already done so, invite a few others to work through this book with you.

Now I invite you to make yourself a cup of tea or coffee, find a comfy seat, and begin to immerse yourself in His Word. As you do, you will come face-to-face with the One who loves you more than you could ever imagine.

Wisdom's Call

Read Proverbs 9:10. What is the foundation for wisdom, and who gives understanding?

Read Proverbs 2:1-6. How do we find wisdom, and who gives it?

CHOOSE WISELY, LIVE FULLY

Read Proverbs 1:1-6 from The Message:

> These are the wise sayings of Solomon,
>   David's son, Israel's king—
> Written down so we'll know how to live well and right,
>   to understand what life means and where it's going;
> A manual for living,
>   for learning what's right and just and fair;
> To teach the inexperienced the ropes
>   and give our young people a grasp on reality.
> There's something here also for seasoned men and women,
>   still a thing or two for the experienced to learn—
> Fresh wisdom to probe and penetrate,
>   the rhymes and reasons of wise men and women.

The Bible is our manual for living. What will you do to more closely follow this manual?

CHAPTER 2

WISDOM AND FOLLY

But the path of the righteous is like the light of dawn,
That shines brighter and brighter until the full day.
The way of the wicked is like darkness;
They do not know over what they stumble.

—Proverbs 4:18-19

About fifteen years ago, I was listening to a sermon as I cleaned house and was jolted by a seemingly passing statement the pastor made. I don't remember the title of the sermon or its topic; what I do remember is the pastor mentioning the two women of Proverbs: Wisdom and Folly. I was stopped in my tracks and brought to full attention. God was speaking to me and directing me to do a study of Proverbs 1–9. I knew I was supposed to study these two women and contrast their lives. I had no idea at the time how profoundly impactful this study would be.

When we think of a woman in Proverbs, most of us think of the virtuous woman of Proverbs 31. If we are honest, we are intimidated by her and cringe inwardly when she is mentioned. In fact, I want you to be completely candid with yourself: did just mentioning her cause feelings of guilt?

After studying Wisdom and Folly, I realized the Proverbs 31 woman is simply the culmination of a life lived wisely. She is a picture of a woman who consistently made the choices that led to life. She is the role model for all of us who desire to love the Lord and be used by Him in this life.

Have you ever noticed that God personifies Wisdom and Folly in His book on wisdom? As I studied Proverbs 1–9, I unexpectedly began to see the blessings and curses that followed these two women based on the choices they made. I drew a line down the middle of a piece of paper and put Wisdom at the top of one column and Folly at the top of the other. As I read Proverbs, I underlined the verses pertaining to Wisdom with a green pen and the ones relating to Folly with a hot pink pen. Then I made the lists of their corresponding blessings or curses.

After finishing the lists, I was astounded. The choices made by Wisdom and the choices made by Folly created two clear paths. I then wrote the word *Death* at the end of the path followed by Folly and *Life* at the end of the path pursued by Wisdom. (This is an activity you will be asked to do at the end of chapter 4.)

I knew immediately that this was a lesson the girls in our youth group needed to hear. As I mentioned previously, I was teaching in the youth department at the time, and our oldest daughter, Lindsey, was in the ninth grade. I knew this message would be extremely important not only for her to hear but for other young women in high school to hear as well. So I talked to our youth pastor and asked for permission to teach this lesson to our high school girls.

As I prayed about how to present these truths, I thought about how our choices are reflected in how we dress, how we carry ourselves, and how we communicate, including our language and even the expressions on our faces. So I purchased several fashion magazines and selected pictures of modestly dressed, confident-looking young women. I also selected some pictures of immodestly dressed or seductive-looking young women. I had decided that after teaching these truths, and displaying the two paths, I would challenge our teens to choose the path of Wisdom and life and to reflect that choice in how they represent Christ.

To test my idea, I sat down with my youngest daughter, Bethany, who was in the third grade at the time. I asked Bethany to make a judgment about these young women in the pictures by the way they were dressed. I asked her to tell me who she thought loved Jesus and who didn't. Without hesitation, she went through picture-by-picture saying, "She loves Jesus. She doesn't love Jesus," based solely on how the girls were dressed. Isn't it amazing that children clearly see right and wrong while we adults try to muddy the water?

I've often heard that we have about twenty seconds to make a first impression. If that is true, what kind of judgment do people make about you when they first meet you? If you claim to be a Christ-follower, would they know it by how you dress and conduct yourself?

Obviously, just because you are dressed modestly doesn't automatically mean you love Christ; nor does it mean that if you dress provocatively you aren't a Christian. But as followers of Christ, our dress and behavior should not deny Him. If it does, it may mean we are on the path that leads to death without even realizing it. We can be so influenced by culture that we lose touch with what is true.

> *There are two paths before you; you may take only one path.* One doorway is narrow. *And one door is wide.* Go through the narrow door. For the wide door leads to a wide path, and the wide path is broad; the wide, broad path is easy, and the wide, broad, easy path has many, many people on it; but the wide, broad, easy, crowded path leads to death. Now then that narrow door leads to a narrow road that in turn leads to life. It is hard to find that road. Not many people manage it. (Matthew 7:13-14 The Voice)

The Bible is clear that there are two paths. Jesus taught about them often. There is the broad path leading to death that many travel (Matthew 7:13), and there is the narrow path that leads to life that He said few would find (v. 14).

The economy of the spirit is so different than that of the natural. The broad path that is so appealing actually leads to a life of bondage and constriction. But the narrow gate opens up to life and freedom in Christ that can only be experienced and never fully imagined.

When we are saved, and we choose to obey God's command to love the Lord with our whole heart, we gain a brand new value system. The value system of the world is turned upside down and inside out. We become small to be exalted; we die to live; we give to receive; we serve;

and we choose the lowest place so that God might use us and move us to a higher place for His glory. Yes, it is radical and it is countercultural. Yes, it goes against every fiber of our flesh, but that is why we must die to our old way of living so that we might come alive to new life in Christ Jesus.

We are choosing either life or death with each decision we make. The idea that our decisions affect only us is a lie. Sin ensnares not only the sinner but also those in its wake. We are all leaving a legacy of life or death, blessings or curses (Deuteronomy 30:19).

When we step back and look at the two paths of Proverbs—the blessings of Wisdom and the curses of Folly—we rightfully ask, "Who in their right mind would choose curses, destruction, and death?"

And yet so many of us do just that every day as we choose to go our own way instead of the way of God. When we think we know better than God, when we choose to elevate our reasoning above the truth of Scripture, we are headed down the path that leads to destruction. Not only are we headed down that path, but our choices impact our descendants as well.

As you work through this study, you will be able to examine your own life and answer the question, "Am I a wise woman or a fool?" If you find that you haven't made wise choices in the past, you still have a choice with each new day. This is the gospel! God is willing to forgive and to grant you the wisdom that leads to life.

None of us want to be deceived. No one wants to think he or she is headed down one path only to discover it is the wrong path. We must honestly look at our own choices and follow them to their logical end. God makes it very clear: there are only two paths. On which path are you?

Herein lies our responsibility to choose wisely. We impact those who follow us. How are our actions and decisions impacting their lives? What kind of example are we? Whether you have biological daughters or spiritual daughters, you have young women to disciple. I started by discipling my daughters and their friends. I currently disciple young women in my home on Thursday mornings. All of us need these truths, regardless of our age.

Christ commanded us to "go and make disciples" (Matthew 28:19-20). How are you doing? Most of us want to obey this command but struggle with knowing how to do it.

Use this book as a launching pad. It is a place to start with vital lessons for women to ensure that they choose the path that leads to life—a path that will fill them with godly confidence, self-worth, purpose, and direction. The truths we examine will also serve as warning signs so that we don't listen to the lies of the evil one and forfeit the "good" plans (Jeremiah 29:11 NLT) that God has for us.

People are not discipled from a pulpit. They are taught, encouraged, and challenged from the pulpit, but they are not held accountable for what they are doing with what God has revealed. Most of us need accountability and relationship to enable us to make the changes necessary to obey God's Word and respond to His call.

If all you are doing is attending church on a Saturday night or Sunday morning, you are probably not growing in your walk with Christ. To not be going forward is to be going backwards. There is no standing still in the Christian life. "Yet they did not obey or incline their ear, but walked in their own counsels and in the stubbornness of their evil heart, and went backward and not forward" (Jeremiah 7:24).

If you are a believer, you have received a great treasure! This treasure of faith is not meant for you alone. It is meant for your children and your children's children, both biological and spiritual. So, I encourage you today to "choose life in order that you may live, you and your descendants" (Deuteronomy 30:19).

Wisdom's Call

Read Proverbs 1–9. Highlight or underline the blessings associated with Wisdom and the curses associated with Folly. Use a different color for each.

Read through Proverbs 1–9 several times as you read this book. Read the chapters in a different translation. Mark or underline repeated phrases or words. Your love for Christ is evidenced by the amount of time you spend in His Word and prayer. Obey the greatest command of all—to love Him with all your heart, soul, mind, and strength (Mark 12:30)—and He will reveal Himself to you. How would you rate your love for Christ?

If you will set your heart on God, He will open your mind.

CHAPTER 3

Choose

These are the wise sayings of Solomon,
David's son, Israel's king—
Written down so we'll know how to live well and right,
to understand what life means and where it's going;
A manual for living,
for learning what's right and just and fair;
To teach the inexperienced the ropes
and give our young people a grasp on reality.

—Proverbs 1:1-4 MSG, emphasis added

Choices—our lives are the product of our choices. My daughter Lindsey described some people's view of life as being somewhat like a game show. The host of the show stands beside the contestant while she stares at two doors. She does not know what is behind door number one or door number two; she has no idea what the outcome of opening either door will be. She thinks her fate relies on guesses, luck, and wishful thinking. Though it is true we do not know what each day will bring, Christ-followers can navigate life with much more certainty than this.

God has made it very clear from the beginning of the Bible that our choices carry consequences. In Genesis 3 Eve chose to disobey God, for God said, "From the tree of the knowledge of good and evil you shall not eat, for in the day that you eat from it you will surely die" (Genesis 2:17). God was clear in His command: *If* you eat from the tree, *then* you will die.

The devil tempted Eve to doubt God's Word and His character. Satan lied and told her that she would not die, but that she would be like God, knowing good and evil. Satan hates God and thus hates those created in God's image. Consequently, Satan's goal is to destroy us by tempting us to deny God as we deny God's Word.

Try as we may, we can't prevent the if/then consequences. However, we can pretend they don't exist or deny they are true, as the enemy, our flesh, and the world (James 3:15) tempt us to do. But an honest person who examines the Scriptures and then honestly examines his or her own life as well as history, will be forced to conclude that God's Word is true and that it never fails.

God put certain spiritual laws into place that are as certain as physical laws. We are all aware of the physical law of gravity. I can deny that it exists and even sincerely believe that I can defy it. But if I jump out of a ten-story building, the law of gravity will determine my outcome—death.

God's spiritual laws are as definite and undeniable as His physical laws. He has told us "the wages [or payoff] of sin is death" (Romans 6:23). Yet so many people think they will "beat the system" or that God is so merciful that He will just overlook their sin.

My husband shared a message with our staff recently, and he titled it, "The Law That Will Not Bend." He taught on Galatians 6:7, "Do not be deceived, God is not mocked; for whatever a man sows, this he will also reap." This law is irrevocable and is profoundly impacting your life, whether you are aware of it or not. This is one of the truths I mentioned in the Introduction that is intertwined in the warp and woof of life. If you are generous, generosity will be given to you. If you are faithful to sow thoughts and words of encouragement, you will be encouraged. If you will ask the Lord to make you aware of your own actions and evaluate them in light of this truth, you will be awestruck at the implications for you and all you influence.

Many people are frustrated because they are waiting for a harvest that they didn't plant. It would be as ridiculous as me planting cactus seeds and expecting flowers to come up. I might be sincere and plant the seed just right in the right amount of fertilized soil. I can water the seeds and watch for them to grow. But it does not matter how sincere I am. If I planted cactus, I will get cactus.

If you are planting negativity, you will reap negativity. If you are selfish, you will not reap generosity. Jesus said, "It is more blessed to give than to receive" (Acts 20:35). Many of the words of Christ seem backwards to the natural man. But God's truth is not backwards, the world is! *Satan has so twisted and perverted the Word of God to appeal to our sin nature that many of us are unable to discern the truths from the lies.*

In addition to the spiritual laws, God has also given us relational laws. He has told us that He created us male and female. He also created the gift of sex to be "unwrapped" and enjoyed only in marriage between one man and one woman (Genesis 2:24). We can choose to try to redefine marriage, or exploit the gift of sex outside of marriage, but we will pay the consequences of breaking God's laws.

We see these truths evident from the beginning of time. Eve ate from the tree and gave the fruit to Adam. They died first spiritually and ultimately physically. But their choices didn't just affect them, they also affected their children. Death entered their family as their own son murdered his brother.

We will find as we study Scripture and our own families that our choices have a ripple effect. Each choice has a consequence for good or evil. In Deuteronomy 28–30, Moses relayed to the Israelites the commands of God. He also went back over what God said would happen if they disobeyed His Word. If you disobey, then these curses will follow (Deuteronomy 28). If you obey, then these blessings will follow you and your lineage.

After going back through all the commands and warnings, Moses told the people: "I have set before you life and death, the blessing and the curse. So choose life in order that you may live, you and your descendants" (Deuteronomy 30:19).

That same choice is ours. We make choices every day. Often we do so without any thought about the consequences. We make hasty decisions based on our own reasoning or feelings at the moment. What we fail to do is follow our choices to their logical conclusion based on the Word of God—a fatal mistake that leads to great heartache and pain.

I once met with a young woman at the request of her mother. She had not been living as a Christ-follower should. She had fallen back into living as if she were single, and her husband had moved out. As I listened to her story and asked a few questions, I realized she wanted a quick fix to get her husband back without any change or accountability on her part. She was trying to live her life in denial of God's Word and didn't understand why she was reaping heartache and relational destruction.

Did you notice the Scripture at the beginning of this chapter? It stated that these proverbs would "give our young people a grasp on reality" (Proverbs 1:4 MSG). There is no reality apart from God and His Word. We are so easily deceived, and our thoughts can be effortlessly manipulated by the evil one. The only way we can have a firm grasp on reality—and I would go even further: to think sanely—is to study and live out God's Word.

The Bible is full of examples of those who sought to live life apart from God and His Word. Look at the legacy or lineage of Adam. In Genesis 4 and 5 you will find the lineages of Cain and Seth. Seth was the son given to Adam and Eve after the death of Abel.

Trace the lineage of Cain from Adam for seven generations, and you will come to Lamech, who was the first recorded polygamist and a murderer (Genesis 4:17-24). But if you trace the lineage of Seth seven generations from Adam (5:3-24), you will find Enoch, who "walked with God; and he was not, for God took him" (v. 24).

In the lineage of Cain you find out what happens when people choose to live their lives apart from God. Cain was defiant and rebelled against God and His commands. His descendants followed suit. Cain lived the way Lady Folly is depicted in Proverbs and was angry that he was reaping the consequences.

It was during the time of Seth that people "began to call upon the name of the LORD" (Genesis 4:26). Seth's legacy was one of blessing. His descendants walked with God. Seven generations from Adam through Seth is Enoch, who so pleased God that He took Enoch so that he did not experience physical death (Genesis 5:24).

We have all inherited a legacy of either blessings or curses. I was incredibly blessed to be born into a Christian family, but not just any Christian family—to a couple who sought to obey God and His Word. And God blessed their desire. God granted my parents three daughters, of whom I am the oldest. All three of us love the Lord and have husbands and children who love Him as well.

Hear me when I say *we are not perfect*! We have experienced pain and struggles in marriage and child-rearing. But God is and has been faithful! Every family on earth is dysfunctional because we are all sinners. Yet God has not left us to figure life out alone or to wander without direction. He has sought us for relationship and revealed Himself through His Word and His Son that we might have life abundant—full and free! He has not left us as orphans but has sent His Spirit to indwell all who repent and call upon Him for salvation. He also desires to use us to point other people to Him and to point the way through the small gate onto the narrow path that leads to life!

The good news is that by choosing Jesus, you can change your lineage and leave a legacy of blessing for your descendants. By repenting and turning to Christ, you can leave the path of curses and death and walk the path that leads to wisdom and life. Salvation is so much more than a ticket to heaven. The abundant life is for today, not just for eternity. If we surrender to God's good will, we will have the greatest victory.

God has a plan for your life, and He desires to reveal it to you. My greatest satisfaction stems from my relationship with God, and my greatest joy is when He speaks to me through His Word and His Spirit and uses me for His glory. Now don't get me wrong, I love my husband, children, and grandchildren, and I derive great pleasure from my relationships with them. In fact, I often tell them I love them so much it almost takes my breath away! But they cannot eclipse the "joy inexpressible" (1 Peter 1:8) that I experience in His manifest presence. This joy cannot be contained—the jump up and down kind of joy that restores childlike wonder and awe to life.

One example of when I experienced God speaking and directing me was when I was preparing to speak at a women's prison several years ago. I couldn't decide what I should share. I prayed and studied and listened for the voice of the Holy Spirit. I finally just *settled* on a message I thought to be suitable. But in my hotel room, just moments before I was to leave for the prison, I was on my knees still wrestling with God over my topic. Almost instantly, the Lord gave me the message I was to share: the two choices in Scripture.

God's Word is very clear about the two choices—we either obey or disobey. There really is no gray. With each choice I am either obeying God and His Word, or denying Him by choosing to go my own way, the way of my flesh or the devil. Almost instantly, I saw all of Scripture boiled down to these two paths. It was as though the two trees of the garden of Eden hovered over every page of Scripture: the tree of life and the tree of the knowledge of good and evil. One represents life, and the other represents death.

As I shared these truths with the women in the prison, they began to see clearly that even if they had inherited a lineage like Cain's, by choosing Christ they could be transferred to the lineage of the blessed. They could become joint heirs with Christ through salvation and could begin their own legacy of blessing! Many of them committed their pasts to Christ and trusted Him for the future that only He can give.

Could it really be that simple? Yes! It is simple but not free—it cost God His only Son (John 3:16). Christ has made the way for us to leave the lineage of Cain behind and to choose the lineage of the blessed. Your family line may be dark and treacherous, with enough pain and dysfunction to baffle many a counselor. But the Wonderful Counselor can heal your soul in salvation and start you down the path of Lady Wisdom that will be a blessing to all who come behind you.

God has been very clear about His commands for life and how He created us to live. So please stay committed to this study and ask the Lord to give you ears to hear and eyes to see His path, the one He has marked out for you.

I know there will be those who will ask the "grace" question: "But, I thought we were saved by grace through faith and are no longer living under the law." Yes, but as Paul so eloquently stated before King Agrippa, "I began in Damascus, then continued in Jerusalem, then throughout the Judean countryside, then among the outsiders—telling everyone they must turn from their past and toward God and **align their deeds and way of life with this new direction**" (Acts 26:20 The Voice, emphasis added). Or as the NIV states it, "I preached that they should repent and turn to God and *demonstrate their repentance by their deeds*" (emphasis added). We are saved by faith, but it is a faith that works.

As Oswald Chambers said,

> You did not do anything to achieve your salvation, but you must do something to exhibit it. You must "work *out* your own salvation" which God has worked *in* you already (Philippians 2:12). Are your speech, your thinking, and your emotions evidence that you are working it "out"? If you are still the same miserable, grouchy person, set on having your own way, then it is a lie to say that God has saved and sanctified you.[1]

We must also acknowledge that we live in a fallen world. Even though we sow the right seed and make wise choices, there will still be times when we will encounter an illness or a broken relationship that is not totally dependent upon us. Life will never be perfect on this planet. And it seems that our dearest and most impacting lessons are learned in the valleys and not on the mountaintops. Jesus said, "In the world you have tribulation, but take courage; I have overcome the world" (John 16:33).

I am not a proponent of health and wealth theology. God is not a genie that we rub just the right way and we get what we want. Our prayers do not manipulate God and we don't obey just to get what we want. We obey to get more of Him!

You can be sure the Creator has given us the truths we need to navigate our way to Him. These are the truths we will be uncovering in this study that I pray you will incorporate into your life and then pass on to others.

When we face hardship or persecution, we can be like Paul and Silas in the Philippian jail and find ourselves singing and praising God, because we have been sowing faith in Christ by our actions and attitudes. Consequently, nothing will be able to defeat you and when you leave this life either through the doorway of death or in the rapture, it will be gain for you! ("To live is Christ, and to die is gain" Philippians 1:21.)

Wisdom's Call

Based on your choices, what kind of lineage do you think you are leaving your descendants?

"His own iniquities will capture the wicked, and he will be held with the cords of his sin" (Proverbs 5:22). The word for "cords" as defined in the Hebrew/Greek Key Study Bible can also be "noose." Thus, we "hang" ourselves with our own sin. How have you seen the consequences of sin in your own life?

CHOOSE WISELY, LIVE FULLY

Read Hebrews 12:1-2. Name the sin that entangles you: _____.
The more you love Christ and fix your eyes on Him, you will find the sin
that once entangled you will no longer even entice you! *When my love for
Christ surpasses my love for self then sin will be defeated!*

The wicked will be snared by their own wrongdoing.
    Their flaws will tie their own hands, *and they will be dragged
through life* by the cords of their sins.

—Proverbs 5:22 The Voice

CHAPTER 4

REAL WISDOM

*It was by wisdom that the Eternal fashioned the earth
and by understanding that He designed the heavens.*

—Proverbs 3:19 The Voice

Proverbs is known as wisdom literature. It reinforces what we know is true from the Creation account in Genesis—God created the world through wisdom. The Bible tells us that this wisdom is a person—Jesus Christ (Hebrews 1:1-2). He is the Wisdom and Word of God. He was present at Creation; all that came to be was created by Him, and He "upholds all things by the word of His power" (vv. 3-4).

Because God created the heavens and the earth by His wisdom and in His order, He created the world to work according to His plan. Wisdom recognizes and chooses to live according to that plan.

Genesis is the foundation, and God as revealed through Jesus Christ, has not changed (Hebrews 13:8.) The patterns, the foundations, the way God has chosen to reveal Himself since the beginning of time as we know it has not been altered. God laid the foundation, the parameters, and the principles for all of life. These principles have been continued throughout all of Scripture and are imperative for human flourishing, purpose, and satisfaction for our lives today.

However, our sin separates us from God and His wisdom. Adam and Eve rebelled against God's Word, and thus we are all held captive by sin. Eve listened to the voice of the evil one and believed she could have knowledge and wisdom apart from God. So, sin entered the world, and we have all experienced its impact.

The sin nature that we have inherited makes it impossible for us to "see" God's plan and to live accordingly. Our reasoning is skewed by sin, and our hearts are "more deceitful than all else" and "desperately sick" (Jeremiah 17:9). We have awareness that there is a God evidenced in nature and our conscience (Romans 1:18-20), but our propensity toward sin causes us to deny and repress the truth.

We are told in Scripture that God requires us to "walk humbly with [our] God" (Micah 6:8). To be humble is not to think too poorly of ourselves because then we make bad decisions. But the converse is true as well. When we think too highly of ourselves and become arrogant, we make wrong decisions. So the key is to not focus on self but to focus on Christ. This emphasis is the essence of humility. Truly He is the only one who can meet our every need and give us the stability, security, and significance from which we make God-honoring decisions.

As we examine our lives and begin to recognize our own destructive choices, we understand we have not been living according to the Creator's instructions. It is somewhat like purchasing an item that must be assembled. You are to follow the directions included in the package, but how often do we barge right ahead trying to assemble it without reading them? And if for some reason the item doesn't work properly, we are directed not to return it to the place of purchase but to the manufacturer. Why? Because it could be operator error instead of a defect in the product. Obey the directions—follow the instructions!

Just as Adam and Eve hid from God and covered themselves with fig leaves to hide their bodies from each other, our relationships are marred by separation. We must enter into a personal relationship with Christ and be healed vertically before we can experience wholeness in our relationships horizontally.

Take marriage, for example. I am by nature a very strong-willed individual. So is my husband. When we married, we were starry-eyed twenty-two year olds, believing our love would surpass any problems we would face. Ten years, three children, graduate school, seminary, and two churches later, I found myself frustrated and disillusioned. I just couldn't get my husband to cooperate with my idea of how our marriage and family were supposed to work. It didn't matter how much I ranted or how many tears I shed, we were at a stalemate. I had become the "nagging spouse" in Proverbs (21:9 MSG). I cried out to God, "Lord, how did I get here, and why isn't life 'working' the way I think it should?"

I had been praying that the Lord would capture my heart and that I would long for Him as a deer pants for water (Psalm 42:1). As my longing for intimacy with the Lord was growing, so was my desire for His Word. I am an avid reader and had been reading some of the works of Watchman Nee. His book *The Release of the Spirit* had revolutionized my understanding of the Spirit-filled life.

Browsing the shelves of a Christian bookstore, I came upon another book by Nee entitled, *Spiritual Authority*. I must confess, I would never have been drawn to a book by that title. It had to have been the Holy Spirit who directed me to pick up the book and purchase it.

Once I opened the book, I could not put it down. As I read the book and worked through the Scriptures and what God had to say about authority, I was accosted by my sin and the rebellion in my own heart. I found myself weeping in repentance. I reflected back over my teen years, past relationships, work experiences, and now my marriage and saw my responsibility for much of the discord and pain.

I met my husband at the door that afternoon as He came into the house and asked him to forgive me. I was obviously so moved emotionally that he was frightened and wanted to know what had me so concerned. As I poured out my heart, I saw him soften, and we both knew the Lord was at work.

I wish I could tell you that I conquered my rebellion in one fell swoop, but it wasn't that easy. I am so thankful the Lord opened my eyes and made me aware of my compulsion to go my own way. I did not want the result of my rebellion to impact my marriage or our children. I certainly didn't want to be a Christ-follower who dishonored Him by being an inaccurate reflection of His character, stumbling down the dark path and hurling headlong into destruction.

Repentance and obedience precede further revelation. As I continued to seek the Lord through His Word and prayer, He continued to gently peel back the layers of my self-deception and enabled me to confess my sin and receive His forgiveness.

Let me stop here and insert a word about marriage to those of you who have children or are discipling young believers. I told our children, and I tell young, single women now, that I will point out to them any red flags or potential problems that I might notice in their dating relationships before they walk down the aisle. But once they walk down the aisle and enter into a covenant with their new spouse and God, I will become their spouse's greatest fan. I will choose to build up and not tear down. The sacred covenant of marriage is not to be entered into lightly. Pray with these young women and seek the Lord with them for His will.

The fear of the Lord upon which wisdom is built is a reverential awe of God that leads to a desire to obey. This desire to obey leads to further revelation and understanding. The path of life grows brighter and brighter as we continue to choose God's way instead of our own (Proverbs 4:18).

I recently met with a young woman who had concerns about a young man who was pursuing her. He had been unfaithful to his previous fiancée. After breaking off his engagement, he started attending the church that she attended. He told her he was a new believer in Christ. He seemed to show up to activities where he knew she would be present. He brought her flowers, was very attentive, and appeared to be sincere.

My counsel to her was to break off all communication and to let him know that he needed to pursue his personal relationship with Christ and to grow spiritually since he was a new believer. I suggested she tell him to not contact her for six months and see if he would abide by it. If the young man was sincere, she would be able to tell by his behavior and respect for her wishes. If he was only pretending, then the Lord would expose that as well.

Young men with less than honorable intentions will oftentimes pursue a young woman just to conquer her. There are people with codependent personalities who will do whatever it takes to win you over only to turn into controllers and sometimes even abusers. Seek the Lord first and foremost. Allow your need for intimacy to be met in your personal relationship with Christ, so you are not so vulnerable to someone with an agenda. The only man you must have is Jesus!

If you are passionately pursuing Christ, you may look to the left or right. If there is a young man pursuing Christ as passionately as you are, then pray about dating him. Do not settle for less than God's good and perfect will (Hebrews 12:2). It does not mean that your relationship will be perfect. But if you seek Christ together, you will be able to face the trials and difficulties of this life with Him as your guide.

God tells us clearly what it takes to please Him and to know Him in Hebrews 11:6: "And without faith it is impossible to please Him, for he who comes to God must believe that He is and that He is a rewarder of those who seek Him." If we will just believe and focus on seeking God, He will reward our seeking with more of Him (Jeremiah 29:13).

My job is not to be great for God but to believe and to seek. The wise woman seeks wisdom (Proverbs 2:3-5) and discerns the very knowledge of God. If I will believe that He is, and that He is a rewarder of those who seek Him, then I will get to know Him; and the better I know Him, the greater I will believe.

The ultimate fulfillment of wisdom and the only one to live perfectly by God's wisdom is Jesus. There is no wisdom apart from Him. As Jonathan Akin said in his book, *Preaching Christ from Proverbs*, "The only way we can heed the practical advice in Proverbs 10–31 is if Proverbs 1–9 has led us into a personal relationship with the Wisdom of God who is Jesus Christ."[1]

My prayer for you is that you would know Christ and walk with Him intimately. It is through wholehearted devotion to Him that life begins to make sense, and you are allowed to "see" what had been veiled before. God is good. He desires to bless His children. When the Bible uses the word *blessed* it can also be translated "happy." You will not find true happiness apart from Christ.

As Randy Alcorn wrote in his book, *Happiness*, "When we seek holiness at the expense of happiness or happiness at the expense of holiness, we lose both the joy of being holy and the happiness birthed by obedience. God commands holiness, knowing that when we follow his plan, we'll be happy."[2]

The sin that promises to make us happy only leads to bondage and pain. The thief really has come to "steal, kill and destroy" (John 10:10). But Christ has come that you might have life abundant! Don't miss the blessings by thinking you can figure life out on your own.

We are going to begin to work through the blessings associated with the path of Wisdom in the next chapters. We will also be looking at the path that leads to curses and death that Folly beckons us to join. Remember God's Word really is our manual for living.

Ask the Holy Spirit to reveal any rebellion in your heart that you have been justifying or rationalizing. As my dear instructor Watchman Nee wrote: "May God be gracious to us by delivering us from rebellion. Only after we have known God's authority and learned obedience can we lead His children in the straight path."[3]

Wisdom's Call

Look back at Proverbs 1–9. Making a column for Wisdom and a column for Folly, record the blessings under Wisdom and the curses under Folly. In the next chapter we will begin working through the blessings associated with Wisdom. Each chapter will highlight one blessing and its obvious contrast reflected in the life of Folly.

Wisdom   **Folly**

"Hence a person who is filled with Christ must be one who is also filled with obedience."

—Watchman Nee

CHAPTER 5

SECURITY

But he who listens to me shall live securely
And will be at ease from the dread of evil.

—Proverbs 1:33, emphasis added

Then you will walk in your way securely
And your foot will not stumble.

—Proverbs 3:23, emphasis added

At this point in the book, we will begin to discover the blessings in Proverbs that are associated with Wisdom. As we delve into each of these blessings, we will also look at their opposite, which will be the curse associated with Folly. We have seen that there really are only two choices or paths to take. Which path will you choose? To which voice will you listen?

The first blessing we will explore is *security*. All of us long for it. We don't like uncertainty in relationships, our jobs, or our future; this longing for security and control grips our minds and can hijack our emotions. Feeling out of control spawns fear and can catapult us into irrational thoughts and actions. But real security is only found in Christ. He is the Rock upon which we build our lives.

Most women struggle with insecurity. For many of us, one of our most difficult struggles with insecurity is in the area of our physical appearance. As one physician who specializes in eating disorders notes:

> Currently, 80 percent of women in the U.S. are dissatisfied with their appearance. And more than 10 million are suffering from eating disorders.... As a result of both genetic and environmental factors, body image issues and eating disorder behaviors may be passed down from generation to generation. This concept, recently labeled "thin-heritance," explores how a mother's views about food, dieting practices, and negative attitudes and comments about her own body or her child's appearance increase her children's risk for poor body image and eating disorders.[1]

My daughter Lindsey conducted an informal survey using a survey website and found that 59 percent of the respondents listed either body, weight, or appearance as their top insecurity—and these were believers.

How is this insecurity impacting our children? They pick up on our attitudes and body image. Are we teaching coping skills and dependence on the Lord to our children, or are we modeling anxiety, stress, and insecurity?

In Carolyn Coker Ross's blog she reports:

- According to the National Eating Disorders Association, 42 percent of first- to third-grade girls want to lose weight, and 81 percent of 10-year-olds are afraid of being fat.

- According to *Teen* magazine, 35 percent of girls ages 6 to 12 have been on at least one diet, and 50 to 70 percent of normal-weight girls think they are overweight.[2]

Do those statistics alarm you as much as they do me? Take a look at some of the characteristics of insecure women listed below. This list was compiled from various sites and books as I researched as well as my own observation. This is not a scientific list but one based on common sense. Do you currently struggle in any of these areas? Has insecurity manifested itself in your life through any of these behaviors?

- Control freak—anxious and uptight; tries to control people and circumstances;

- Arrogant—looks down on others;

- Fearful—afraid of speaking in front of a group, of being yourself for fear of rejection, or of really trusting God;

- Jealous—envious of your spouse or another person;

- Seductive—the more skin you reveal the greater the level of insecurity;

- Lack of eye contact—unable to connect by directly looking at others;

- People pleaser—stretch yourself way too thin by making too many commitments because you can't say no.

- Defensive—cannot take constructive criticism;

- Materialistic—must have the latest purse, designer label, car, or live in a certain neighborhood;

- Perfectionist—won't attempt anything you can't do well or perfect, fear of failure;

- Critical—tear down instead of building up.

Do you recognize yourself in any of these descriptions? *We become self-absorbed when we are insecure.* Focusing on self increases our anxiety and need for control. The antidote is to trust Christ and begin to look out instead of in.

Do you walk into a room or a meeting as an ambassador of Christ, on mission for Him? Or do you walk in focused on yourself and wondering who will notice you or make you feel comfortable? Ask God to use you to encourage someone else. When you focus outward, you have a God-confidence that draws others to you.

There are times we all deal with insecurity. Last year, I weighed myself after the Christmas holidays. Need I say more? I love to bake! I got that from my mother. We tease her and tell her that her freezer grows cakes. If someone needs a dessert for a special occasion, she says, "I'll just get one out of my freezer." In fact, my two sisters and I have all requested that she leave her freezer to us in her will.

So here was my Christmas conundrum last year. I really like sugar cookies and am always on a quest for the best sugar cookie recipe. I tried way too many recipes over the holidays and then found myself paying for it in January by trying to get rid of my unwanted winter coat. Now I can become discouraged and depressed about my added weight and feel insecure because of it; or I can pray, devise a plan, and through the power of the Holy Spirit and accountability stick with that plan to lose the unwanted weight. The extra pounds will come off if I continue to make wise choices and stay away from sugar cookies!

Don't listen to the accuser of the brethren. The evil one will go after your Achilles heel. He is not omniscient, but he does know our weaknesses from observation. Take it to the Lord in prayer, and seek God's Word to battle the fiery darts of the evil one. Most of us know from experience what researchers have discovered about insecurity. "Failure to cope with insecurity could have a negative effect on your relationships and your career and can also lead to depression."[3]

Most feelings of insecurity are coupled with thoughts such as these:

> "I can't do this."
> "I don't fit in."
> "Will my husband be faithful to me?"
> "I will never get over my insecurity."

Oh how often and easily thoughts such as these bombard our minds! As Renee Swope said in her book, *A Confident Heart*, "Sometimes we agree with them and they become our own. These are the voices of insecurity that cast shadows of doubt over our perspective and keep us from becoming the women we want to be—the women God created us to be."[4]

It is high time we get over ourselves. This life is not about us anyway! What God desires is a vessel fully surrendered to Him that He might do what only He can accomplish. Then He gets all the glory, and our faith is strengthened as we watch Him work.

I was reading in a devotional recently and was challenged by this thought from Evan Hopkins, "God's commands are assurances of power.

He knows we cannot make ourselves strong. What He requires is, that we should be willing to be made strong. Allow yourself to be empowered. You have no ability, but I have given you capacity. Your weakness and emptiness and need are your capacity to receive."[5]

You have the capacity to receive from the Lord everything you need to fulfill His plan for your life. The weakness of our flesh leads to the doubt that holds us captive and prevents us from experiencing all that Jesus Christ died to purchase for us on Calvary. The good news of the cross is that Satan was defeated, and we now have the power of the Holy Spirit living within us to enable us to be secure in our calling and secure in His Word.

One morning as I was driving to my Bible study group, I began to reflect on John 11. This is the passage where Jesus raised Lazarus from the dead. As I was envisioning what that moment must have been like, I suddenly had an overwhelming sense of God's presence. I felt the Lord impressing upon my heart that just as He called Lazarus from the grave and commanded the people to unwrap him and set him free, God is more than able to call us by name and set us free. You may *feel* that your insecurity is insurmountable, but I want to remind you that feelings are not truth. Let me repeat myself, *feelings are not truth*!

Our feelings seem to live on the front row of our lives. There are times when our feelings are so strong they seem to take over our minds. At that moment we must begin to live out the instruction in 2 Corinthians 10:3-5. We must take these errant feelings, coupled with wrong ways of thinking, and refuse them entrance into our minds. We take them captive. Then we must replace them with the truth of God's Word:

> For though we walk in the world, we do not fight according to this
> world's rules of warfare. The weapons of the war we're fighting are
> not of this world but are powered by God and effective at tearing
> down the strongholds *erected against His truth*. We are demolishing

arguments and ideas, every high-and-mighty philosophy that pits itself against the knowledge of *the one true* God. We are taking prisoners of every thought, *every emotion*, and subduing them into obedience to the Anointed One. (2 Corinthians 10:3-5 The Voice)

Did you notice in these verses that these strongholds (wrong ways of thinking) are erected against truth? We must demolish or tear them down through the power of the Holy Spirit and the Word of God.

We have a very real enemy who assaults the truth of God and can manipulate our emotions. That is why we cannot *feel* our way into a new way of acting. Instead, we must think (according to God's Word) and act our way into a new way of feeling. If we will choose to act according to God's Word, eventually our feelings will line up.

Feelings that are fueled by wrong ways of thinking are like ruts in our brain. When I was a child, I had an aunt and uncle who had go-carts they allowed us to ride in their backyard. We rode those go-carts through the yard so often around the same path that we created ruts or tracks. To allow the grass to grow again over these ruts, we had to choose new paths, which eventually would be new ruts.

Similarly, the old ruts in our thinking must be stopped and replaced with truth. As we arrest those wrong thoughts and replace them with truth, we are creating new ruts that will become new habits of thinking and reacting.

These feelings of insecurity will only be conquered when we take God at His Word and believe He is able! Insecurity increases anxiety and gives entrance to the fiery darts of the evil one. These fiery darts are the lies that so often trigger feelings that lead us down the wrong path. It is amazing to me that the more self-focused our society has become, the more anxious and insecure we have become.

The statistics reveal the truth. There has been

an extraordinary trend in mental illness: an increase in the prevalence of reported anxiety disorders of more than 1,200 percent since 1980.

In that year, 2 percent to 4 percent of Americans suffered from an anxiety disorder, according to the American Psychiatric Association's Diagnostic and Statistical Manual (DSM) of Mental Disorders, used by psychiatrists and others worldwide to diagnose mental illness.

In 1994, a study asking a random sample of thousands of Americans about their mental health reported that 15 percent had ever suffered from anxiety disorders. A 2009 study of people interviewed about their anxiety repeatedly for years raised that estimate to 49.5 percent—which would be 117 million U.S. adults.[6]

Did you notice the huge increase in anxiety disorders since 1980? If the 2009 study is accurate, that means half of our population has or is suffering from an anxiety disorder. In fact, Brené Brown in her book, *Daring Greatly*, said, "Americans today are more debt-ridden, obese, medicated, and addicted than we ever have been."[7]

How are we to deal with this alarming trend? Very often, insecurities are the root of our anxiety, and until we deal with the core spiritual issues, we are simply numbing the effects by medicating our feelings. This anxiety will not go away until we deal with our sin issues and believe and act based upon who God says we are in Christ.

We need to face our insecurities. Ephesians 1 reveals the blessings God has granted for those who are "in Christ." Peter tells us we have "become partakers of the divine nature" (2 Peter 1:4). We are "co-heirs with Christ" (Romans 8:17 NIV). We have been granted everything we need for life and godliness (2 Peter 1:3).

When we are given authority and position and privilege in any other area of our lives, it gives us a natural sense of confidence to do the job set before us. It should be the same with our position in Christ. Not to mention

Scripture tells us "He is intimate with the upright" (Proverbs 3:32b). We have been invited to experience intimacy with the Almighty. He desires for us to be part of His plan and His mission. God longs to reveal Himself through Scripture and the Holy Spirit who dwells within us.

First Corinthians 3:1-3 is a rebuke to the Corinthian believers:

> And I, brethren, could not speak to you as to spiritual men, but as to men of flesh, as to infants in Christ. I gave you milk to drink, not solid food; for you were not yet able to receive it. Indeed, even now you are not yet able, for you are still fleshly. For since there is jealousy and strife among you, are you not fleshly, and are you not walking like mere men?

In these verses Paul reprimanded the Corinthians because they were living as "mere men." What were the indicators? Strife and jealousy. What causes strife and jealousy? Insecurity!

We are to derive our identity and security from our position "in Christ." I am not basing my security on how I look, how much I weigh, where I live, what car I drive, or whether I am or am not married. The truth is, I am beloved, chosen, sealed, and a joint heir with Christ, whether I feel like it or not.

I enjoy listening to podcasts. One of my favorite people to listen to is Tim Keller. In his sermon entitled, "A World of Idols," he stated, "A fanatic doesn't love Christ too much, he doesn't love him enough."[8] We would describe a fanatic as one who has become rigid in his or her legalism. Fanatics have lost the balance of grace and holiness. They have missed the balance of Christ. When Christ is enthroned as King in your life, you will have a high view of God and a high view of every person who has been created in His image. Thus, you will not be caught up in strife and jealousy. On the contrary, you will be gracious and loving.

How do we accomplish living in the Spirit instead of the flesh? I know I don't want to live carnally. I want to accurately reflect my Savior. Therefore, I must:

1. Know who I am "in Christ." It is imperative that I know what the Bible says about those who belong to Christ. The more my identity is rooted in God's Word, the less I will be affected by my feelings.

2. Take my thoughts captive to the obedience of Christ (see 2 Corinthians 10:3-5). Nothing the enemy throws at me can defeat me unless I allow it to.

3. Speak and believe God's Word. After my thoughts are taken captive, I must replace them with the truth of God's Word. Sometimes I write Scripture on a note card and tape it to my bathroom mirror or the dash of my car. I want it before me at all times so I can meditate on truth and combat the lie with the sword of the Spirit (Ephesians 6:17).

4. Be on mission to fulfill His purpose! Now that I am being "transformed by the renewing of [my] mind," I will be able to "prove what the *will of God* is, that which is good and acceptable and perfect" (Romans 12:2, emphasis added).

God always calls us out of our comfort zone. He will call you to do things that you cannot do on your own so that He gets all the glory. Why are we amazed? We will experience God's movement and answers to prayer when we choose to believe and say yes to His call on our lives.

I am a follower of the One who can open doors that no one can open and closes doors that no one can close (Revelation 3:7). All He needs is an empty vessel through which to work.

When we look around at the condition of our world and the seemingly unstoppable downward spiral of our culture, it is easy to become discouraged. We do not despair as those who have no hope (1 Thessalonians 4:13) because our lives are built upon the truth of God's Word. The storms will still come, but you will not fall because your life is built upon the foundation of Jesus Christ and His Word (Matthew 7:24-27).

God wants to raise up an army of men and women who say yes to Him. To the God "who is able to do far more abundantly beyond all that we ask or think" (Ephesians 3:20). God works through us to accomplish what only He can do. He is able! Because He is able, I am able!

Wisdom's Call

What are you most insecure about? What Scriptures will you use to replace the lie with the truth?

Read Ephesians 1:1-14. List all of the blessings associated with being "in Christ."
"In Christ" I am…

How are your insecurities impacting your children or those you are discipling? Honestly share your insecurities with an accountability partner or your small group. Ask your partner or group to pray with you as you seek to obey the Lord and place your trust in Him.

Lindsey's Insight

I'm not sure there was a more awkward time in my life than the fifth grade. I was a prepubescent, insecure, uncoordinated girl trying to fit in. Fifth-grade Lindsey was worried about things such as the hair sticking through my panty hose at church, my rapidly growing feet, a lack of athletic ability, and whether or not the cute boy at school noticed me.

These days my insecurities look a bit different, although they still exist. I've struggled with many kinds of insecurities over the years, some funny and shallow and others deep and more extensive.

It seemed all of my past and present insecurities came crashing down on me at once the day I became a mother. As I held my firstborn daughter in my arms, I felt love as I'd never known it before and fear that could smother me in an instant. Twenty-one months after her birth, our second daughter was born. If growing up as a female comes with its own set of insecurities, mothering two females has proven to amplify those insecurities beyond what I could have imagined! I'll never forget the feeling each time the doctor placed my crying, slippery baby onto my chest. While I was overwhelmed with love for each one, that new love was accompanied by a whole new world of fear, insecurity, and doubt.

Would I be a good mother? What effect would my failures and shortcomings have on these girls? How would I teach them to be strong, secure, compassionate women who love the Lord with all of their hearts?

I remember a few months after our first daughter was born, I held her while she slept, studied every aspect of her sweet little face, and cried at the thought of her ever struggling with the person God made her to be. As her mother, it's easy for me to see she is "fearfully and wonderfully made"! (Psalm 139:14). The love I have for my children opened my eyes in a whole new way to the love my Father has for me. His love truly does cast out fear (1 John 4:18).

Not long after becoming a mother I joined a discipleship group my mom led in her home. As we walked through the Bible chronologically over the next year and a half, I began to come to know and love the God of the Bible on a deeper level than ever before. As I came to understand more about His character and His love for me, I was able to slowly let go of many of the insecurities I had allowed to cripple me for years. I began to practice replacing the lies I had believed with truth from God's Word. The Word of God was the key to unlocking the freedom from insecurity I desperately wanted.

Part of my life's mission is to pass on this love for God and His Word to my children. When we come to realize who God is, who He says we are, and what our future holds in Him, we can find true rest, confidence, and peace.

In her book, *Women of the Word*, Jen Wilkin says, "Our insecurities, fears, and doubts can never be banished by the knowledge of who we are. They can only be banished by the knowledge of 'I AM.' "[9] When we meet the God of the Bible in a real and intimate way, His character and great plan of redemption is more than enough to motivate us to shift our focus.

When I draw near to the Lord, feast on the truth of God's Word, and cast my anxiety and fear on Him in prayer, my cup is filled by the One who made me and loves me unconditionally. I can enter my day boldly as a beloved daughter rather than bask in condemnation, insecurity, and fear. Only then can I teach my own children to do the same.

> Here I stand **secure** and confident
> before all the people; I will praise the Eternal.
> —Psalm 26:12 The Voice, emphasis added

CHAPTER 6

DISCRETION AND UNDERSTANDING

Discretion will guard you,
Understanding will watch over you,
To deliver you from the way of evil,
From the man who speaks perverse things.

—Proverbs 2:11-12

According to *Merriam Webster's Online Dictionary* the word *discretion* means: "the quality of being careful about what you do and say."[1] The Hebrew literally means "meditation, thought, prudence, plan."

Part of the command given to women in 1 Timothy 2 is to be discreet in the way we dress and adorn ourselves. We are to reflect on the outside what we are professing to possess inwardly. So we are not to focus primarily on our outward appearance but on our interior life so that our good works will be seen, which "is proper for women making a claim to godliness" (1 Timothy 2:10). This instruction is given in the context of prayer. Read this passage from The Message translation: "Since prayer is at the bottom of all this, what I want mostly is for men to pray—not shaking angry fists at enemies but raising holy hands to God. And I want women to get in there with the men in humility before God, not primping before a mirror or chasing the latest fashions but doing something beautiful for God and becoming beautiful doing it" (1 Timothy 2:8-10).

Think about some of the women you know who walk with the Lord. They have a vibrant prayer life. They are the very ones you want praying for you when you face a crisis or trial. These women possess a radiant, inward beauty that overshadows the outward. Often times they will not be as concerned with fashion or being culturally relevant, but their God-given wisdom and discretion causes them to be sought out by those who want to know God and walk with Him. These women exude the joy of the Lord, and peace is in their wake. They possess a stability and purpose that is God-given. This is what God values in a woman.

In contrast, the foolish woman focuses on the outer beauty to the neglect of her interior soul. Read what Proverbs 11:22 says about her: "As a ring of gold in a swine's snout / So is a beautiful woman who lacks discretion." But my favorite translation of this verse is the Message: "Like a gold ring in a pig's snout / is a beautiful face on an empty head." None of us want to be an empty-headed fool heading down the path that leads to death.

Discretion and understanding are paired in Scripture. *Understanding* is defined as "the knowledge and ability to judge a particular situation or subject."[2] We need to be able to discern good and evil and then understand which path we need to take to obey God and experience His life.

One of my sisters sent me a poem, and it so perfectly depicts this truth. The title of the poem was, "Autobiography in Five Short Chapters." In chapter one, which is verse one, a person walks down a street and falls into a deep hole. The person moves from pretending not to see the hole to trying to avoid the hole only to find themselves back at the bottom every time. Unfortunately, it takes the person to the fifth chapter to finally decide to walk down another street.[3]

The first time we realize we are on the wrong path and fall into a pit, we must get up—size up the situation and make a wise decision not to go down that path again. The empty-headed woman keeps going down the same path, while the woman of discretion and understanding makes a course correction.

One of my daughters had a friend who kept making the same mistakes in her dating relationships. My daughter was so frustrated that her friend wouldn't heed the truth of God's Word but instead kept heading down the same path and falling into the same pit of sin.

She was falling into this pit because she allowed herself to be led by her feelings. She did whatever made her feel better at the moment. She allowed herself to be deceived. The path that leads to destruction is a dark path paved with anxiety and confusion. When you are on that path you will continue to make wrong choices because you are on the wrong path! Repentance is the only way off the path that leads to destruction.

So often our emotions sabotage our minds. This is when we must cling to God's Word. Speak it. Stand on it. Expect God to move in faithfulness to what He has said. He is faithful and true! Because the wise woman chooses to act on what is true, God will bless her with His presence and wisdom.

Discretion and understanding, and the lack thereof, are evident not only in our actions but also in our speech. Godly people are discreet: they think before they speak. They have great understanding of God's Word and how it relates to specific situations. They always seem to have just the right word for the moment. This is because they know God and His Word. They have sought Him with their whole heart, and He has revealed Himself to them.

My parents are beautiful examples of understanding and discretion. They have consistently followed Christ and pointed others to Him. I am so thankful for them and for every person God has allowed to cross my path who has made me want to know Christ more intimately and follow Him more closely. I am grateful for those who have pointed me to the path that leads to life.

I am also thankful for biblical examples. One example from the Old Testament is Joseph. He was a man whose wisdom and discretion were noticed by others.

Joseph was sold into slavery by his brothers and ended up in the home of Potiphar. He was given favor until he was falsely accused by Potiphar's wife. Suddenly, he found himself in prison. But because Joseph depended upon the Lord, God granted him favor, and he rose to prominence even while in prison. When Pharaoh had two dreams that none of his wise men could interpret, Pharaoh's cupbearer remembered how Joseph had interpreted his dream when he himself was in prison.

God granted Joseph wisdom, and he credited God as being the

revealer of all mysteries. Joseph was rewarded for his discernment and wisdom by being placed in a position second only to Pharaoh.

So Pharaoh said to Joseph, "Since God has shown all of this to you, I can't imagine anyone wiser and more discerning than you. Therefore you will be in charge of my household. All of my people will report to you and do as you say. Only I, because I sit on the throne, will be greater than you. I hereby appoint you head over all of the land of Egypt" (Genesis 41:39-41 The Voice).

Whose guiding hand was protecting and preserving Joseph? God was the one who placed Joseph in Egypt so that he could protect the lineage through which God had promised the Messiah. But Joseph was not privy to the backstory. All he knew was that God had given him a promise in a dream, and his current circumstances did not match the promise. There is no record of Joseph wallowing in self-pity or blaming God for failing him. Instead, Joseph continued to believe and trust even when his circumstances were horrific, and his feelings probably screamed otherwise.

In fact, Joseph was part of the fulfillment of the promise God had given to Abraham in Genesis 15. God told Abraham that his descendants would be in Egypt for four hundred years. Then God promised to raise up a deliverer who would bring the people back to the Promised Land to take possession of what God had promised. God's plan was being fulfilled. Remember one of the truths we emphasized in the introduction: if God has stated it, it is only a matter of time before you should experience it. God had spoken, and He brought it to pass.

Another Old Testament example is Solomon. God appeared to Solomon one night in a dream and said, "Ask what you wish Me to give you" (1 Kings 3:5).

Solomon responded humbly to the Lord and prayed, "So give Your servant an understanding heart to judge Your people to discern between good and evil. For who is able to judge this great people of Yours?" (1 Kings 3:9).

Solomon began his ministry depending upon the Lord. But he would later veer off the path of life and onto the path that leads to death through the influence of wealth and his many wives. The Lord had given instructions for Israel's kings, and Solomon did not obey the word of the Lord that God had given the people through Moses. In Deuteronomy 17, the Lord said,

> He shall not multiply wives for himself, or else his heart will turn away; nor shall he greatly increase silver and gold for himself.
>
> Now it shall come about when he sits on the throne of his kingdom, he shall write for himself a copy of this law on a scroll in the presence of the Levitical priests. It shall be with him and he shall read it all the days of his life, that he may learn to fear the LORD his God, by carefully observing all the words of this law and these statutes, that his heart may not be lifted up above his countrymen and that he may not turn aside from the commandment, to the right or the left, so that he and his sons may continue long in his kingdom in the midst of Israel. (Deuteronomy 17:17-20)

Because Solomon did not obey the command of God, he and his descendants suffered the consequences. During the reign of Solomon's son, Rehoboam, the kingdom was divided. The Northern Kingdom continued to live in rebellion and was taken into captivity by the Assyrians. Although there were brief times of revival in the Southern Kingdom, the people in the south were eventually taken into captivity by the Babylonians because of their rebellious ways and their unwillingness to repent and return to God and His Word.

God was patient and long-suffering with His children in the Northern and Southern Kingdoms. He sent prophet after prophet to confront them with their sin and call them back to God and His Word. But they hardened their hearts and pursued the broad path that leads to destruction, causing them to eventually implode. They lived as the godless nations around them, and God brought upon them all the curses He had warned them about in Deuteronomy 28–30.

Reflect on this insight from *Your Daily Walk Bible*: "When People rebel against God, they end up destroying themselves. They fall by their own wickedness (Proverbs 11:5) and are snared by their own transgressions (29:6). Ponder the timelessness of God's wisdom as you consider the results of abortion, drug and alcohol abuse, broken homes, and homosexuality in our day."[4]

We learn from Solomon that we must remain humble to be wise and understanding. "Pride precedes destruction; an arrogant spirit gives way to a *nasty* fall" (Proverbs 16:18 The Voice). As you come alongside and help others, be careful that you don't become arrogant and fall into your own snare (Galatians 6:1). We have a very real and vicious enemy who "prowls around like a roaring lion, seeking someone to devour" (1 Peter 5:8).

We will do well to take note that this warning is in the context of humbling ourselves "under the mighty hand of God" (1 Peter 5:6). *We must stay little to be used by God in big ways.*

When we were training our children, I would often point to the friends of their older siblings as examples of the two paths. When the Lord was revealing these truths to me, our oldest daughter was entering high school. Her brother had just entered college and some of his friends were already on the path that leads to destruction. By observing their choices, it was evident which path they were pursuing. Several of them self-destructed before they completed their college degrees.

I was not judging these classmates of my son; I was simply observing the fruit of their lives (Matthew 7:16-20). They were reaping at a very young age the seeds they were sowing, and the fruit of their lives made it evident to all who were discerning enough to notice.

Obviously that broke my heart. God has made His commands very clear. He has spelled out for us the blessings that accompany obedience and the curses that are the result of disobedience. My husband, Steve, preached a message recently titled, "The High Cost of Sin," based on Esau trading his birthright for a bowl of soup and a piece of bread (Genesis 25). Steve stated, "We can choose our sin, but we can't choose the consequences."

Most of us close our ears to the truth and instead listen to the voice of our flesh, the world, or the enemy. It takes the work of the Holy Spirit to open our eyes and our ears that we might see and hear as God sees and hears. Genuine repentance will always follow that revelation.

One of the ways to guard against being deceived is to saturate ourselves in the Word of God. Living out the truths in His Word keeps us humble and dependent upon His Spirit. Set some goals in the following areas. Goals that are never set will not be met. We must be intentional to be wise.

Here are some ways to ensure we stay on the path that leads to life:

- Read and memorize Scripture. Have a plan or system to read through the Word of God each year. It will require you to spend about fifteen minutes a day.

- Pray. Grow in your relationship with the Lord by spending time with Him in prayer. Use a prayer notebook. See Appendix E for further instructions.

- Read Christian classics and biographies. I have provided a suggested list in Appendix C.

- Invest in worship music.

- Be actively engaged in discipleship.

- Serve within the local body of Christ and in your community. Be aware of how God is moving in the world, and join Him when He calls upon you to act.

- Pray for missionaries and mission organizations. Support them financially.

- Go on a short-term mission trip.

Join Wisdom and begin to call out the truths of God's Word to those in your sphere of influence. Revere Him and His Word, and you will become a woman of discretion and understanding. Others will seek you out because of your knowledge and ability to judge right from wrong. You will persuade others to join you on the path that leads to life due to the evidence of God's presence and blessing.

Wisdom's Call

Commit to memorize the following Scripture:

> Do not let kindness and truth leave you;
> Bind them around your neck,
> Write them on the tablet of your heart.
> So you will find favor and good repute
> In the sight of God and man.
> Trust in the LORD with all your heart
> And do not lean on your own understanding.
> In all your ways acknowledge Him,
> And He will make your paths straight.

—Proverbs 3:3-6

Who do you depend on for counsel?

What adjustments will you make in your own life to become a woman of discretion and understanding?

Alli's Insight

Discretion and Understanding

> *I have counsel and sound wisdom;*
> *I have insight; I have strength.*
> —Proverbs 8:14

During my senior year of high school, the church my father pastors went through a very difficult time. He followed a long-serving, tenured pastor, and some people who didn't like change challenged his leadership, slandering his name and character. My younger sister and I struggled to love the church where the Lord had placed us. We had just moved there the previous year, and not knowing exactly what was happening or from whom the insults were coming was difficult to say the least. It was easy to question everything and everyone's motives.

One of the most genuine people I've ever met "just happened" to be my Sunday school teacher during my last two years of high school at our new church. I say, "just happened" to be, because I know that in God's perfect providence she was exactly the person I needed during this time. Ashley is the kind of person who seems to always be smiling, yet she is so down to earth and real. It was not uncommon for her to have us over to spend the night in her apartment or meet us for coffee. When my high school boyfriend and I broke up, she put flowers on my desk at work just to cheer me up. This is the kind of person she is.

During all of the hardships of my senior year, Ashley provided constant discretion and understanding. She would listen to my heart's cries and encourage me with Scripture and prayer. Even though I immaturely ran from the Lord during this time, she never faltered in her love for me. She was a safe place, yet I knew she would give me sound wisdom from the Word of God.

Fast forward to several years later when my husband and I found ourselves back at this church for my husband to serve as a pastoral intern. When the high school ministry mentioned needing more Sunday school teachers, we both jumped at the chance. I was privileged to teach a class of eleventh grade girls during our year there, and I thought of sweet Ashley and her influence on my life often. Watching my Sunday school girls grow in the Lord and walk through the difficulties of their teenage years, I saw myself becoming that same source of counsel and wisdom my teachers once were to me. I thank God for the opportunity I was given to pour back into the same church that I once wanted to run from.

I believe that God graciously gives us people in our lives who become sources of godly wisdom and counsel. I also believe that through the study of the Word and memorizing of Scripture, God can use each of us to be those same vessels of service that He flows through if we are willing. Having discretion and understanding with others will deepen our relationships and help us to spur one another on in the faith.

"[Do] something beautiful for God and [become] beautiful doing it."
—1 Timothy 2:10b MSG

CHAPTER 7

SIGNIFICANCE

So you will find favor and good repute
In the sight of God and man.
Trust in the LORD with all your heart
And do not lean on your own understanding.
In all your ways acknowledge Him,
And He will make your paths straight.

—Proverbs 3:4-6

Christian psychologist Larry Crabb has written that all human beings have two very basic needs and desires: to be unconditionally loved and to be truly significant. We want our lives to count, to live with purpose. Crabb goes on to present the case that only Christ can satisfy these two fundamental needs: "In Christ we are at every moment eternally loved and genuinely significant."[1]

Because we so often look to other people or other things to meet these needs, we remain frustrated and unfulfilled. Your spouse will never be able to meet your every need. Every human being will let you down at some point. None of us is perfect. The only perfect person to ever live was Christ. That is why He is the only one capable of knowing us completely and yet loving us eternally.

As we find our significance and security in Christ, we begin to live beyond ourselves. Until we reach this point, we live as beggars. It is as though we are walking around with an empty cup as we look to our husbands, children, friends, jobs, or materialism for significance.

We are constantly seeking worth and significance from other people. When they let us down, we personalize it and begin to think that we have no worth or significance. Only in Christ are we able to live with a Kingdom perspective and live for what will outlive us.

Your relationship with God the Father, through Christ, gives your life significance. You are a joint-heir with Christ and have been written into God's grand narrative. It is "in Christ" that we find our purpose and significance.

Reading through Proverbs we see the guidelines God has given us for living. He has made it very clear. So why do we have a hard time believing or obeying? We are like the Israelites in the Old Testament. The law simply exposed their sin. It does the same thing to us—our sin is the problem. *Our sin is the thief of our significance.*

How many times have you seen a sign that read, "Wet paint, do not touch," and suddenly you have a desire to touch it? Or the speed limit is 55 and you want to drive 60 or 65? Or a sign that reads "Stay off the grass" seems to provoke that little voice that says, "I dare you!" Or, "Says who?" Does your sin nature rear its ugly head as mine does?

This is not learned behavior; we are all born with a sin nature. If you doubt that, work with two-year-olds in the nursery at church one Sunday. Our granddaughter is only nineteen months old and has already determined that she will do exactly what mommy and daddy tell her *not* to do.

This precious child has apparently heard some of us say, "Oh, gosh!" because she has picked it up and is at the age where she repeats everything she hears. But when she says these two words, they sound more like "Oh, God!" So her parents told her not to say that, but instead to say "Oh, my!" or "Oh, goodness!"

After putting her to bed one night, her parents heard her jabbering. Listening in on the monitor they heard her saying, "Oh, gosh! Oh, gosh! Oh, gosh!" over and over. Her dad spoke to her through the monitor and simply said her name. She looked around and then threw her blanket up over her head. In our human nature, when we are caught in our rebellion, we all want to hide.

The next day I went by their house. I walked back to check on her baby brother, and she followed me to his room. She stopped right beside me, and when I looked down at her she grinned mischievously and said, "Oh, gosh!"

Now I have to tell you that as her grandmother, I think she is adorable.

I had to fight laughing out loud. But what is cute in a less than two-year-old is tragic in an adult. It is this sin nature that must be taken to the cross. Sin will steal our significance.

Finding favor with God, as Proverbs 3:4 describes, is dependent upon verses 5 and 6. As The Preacher's Commentary states,

> It begins with commitment. Nothing less than *"with all your heart"* (v. 5) is sufficient. Choices, decisions, motives, intentions must all be directed to what God wants and what God can do. *"Trust"* steps onto the bridge of God's loving power and leaves the shoreline of our own abilities and ambitions behind. Such belief means literally to "bet your life" on God's truth and wisdom.... The path we walk is marked out (directed, v. 6) by Him, and the power to walk is His gift.[2]

Believing who God says we are in Christ grants us the significance we all long for. When we reach the point of "betting our life" on God's truth and wisdom, He begins to reveal His purpose and plan for our lives.

In God's purpose we experience great awe and wonder. How is it that the Creator of the universe not only loves me but desires to be in an intimate relationship with me? This realization leads me to revel in His great love. Once again, time stands still, and I am enthralled with Him! I am changed as I gaze on His holiness.

In God's great love and significance, I find security. I am able to roll my anxieties over onto Him (1 Peter 5:7) and experience life without apprehension or distrust. I begin to experience the meaning, importance, and worth that God designed for me to encounter. But these promises will only become reality when I believe God's Word and begin to live life based upon these truths.

Love makes the difference. We so genuinely love and delight in our grandchildren that they respond to that delight. They are excited when they see us, and they desire to please. Our love for them is not based on their performance but simply in their being.

Just as we learned when we looked at Ephesians 1 that we are blessed with "every spiritual blessing" (v. 3) in Christ Jesus, we understand our blessedness is because we are positionally "in Christ." I am loved because I am accepted through salvation in Jesus Christ. This is a truth too great to ever get over. If we understand that God delights in us and know the great price He paid to set us free from sin, we will respond in awe, wonder, and delight as well as a desire to please and obey!

As Sally Clarkson said in *Own Your Life*, "When we try to reduce God to something we can comprehend or a philosophy we can understand, our souls become numb to His preeminence and transcendence. When we're caught up in the constant activity and responsibilities of adult life, we must learn to consciously open our 'child's' eyes to see the miraculous that surrounds us."[3]

One of the ways modern technology has enriched our lives is the ease with which we can share pictures of current events with those we love. Our children often send us pictures of our grandchildren as they go about their everyday routines. It is so much fun to experience life with them this way. Recently our daughter sent us a picture of her two-year-old eating ice cream. Ruthie's ice cream smeared face was beaming! She was thoroughly enjoying this indulgence.

When was the last time you marveled at God's creation or delighted in an afternoon with a loved one? Every good and perfect gift comes down from the Father (James 1:17). It is "in Christ" that our innocence is restored. In Him we can recapture the astonishment and joy of childhood. Embrace enthusiastically the wonder of being God's beloved!

As we find our significance in Christ, we begin to live beyond ourselves. We are granted a Kingdom perspective and live for what will outlive us. In Him we are able to receive each day as a gift. I encourage you not to wait to celebrate. Capture each moment and be wholly present. Don't miss an opportunity to praise and give thanks to the One who grants us life and meaning.

When we doubt our significance it affects everything about us. When we wallow in self-pity and insecurity we are much more likely to make bad decisions. We have a tendency to listen to our emotions instead of God's Word and His Spirit. We become like Folly, needing others to validate us.

Robert McGee said, "If we base our worth solidly on the truths of God's Word, then our behavior will often reflect His love, grace, and power. But if we base our worth on our abilities or the fickle approval of others, then our behavior will reflect the insecurity, fear, and anger that come from such instability."[4]

Unfortunately, most of us evaluate our self-worth based upon how we perceive others approve or disapprove of us. We must refute the lies of the evil one with the truth of who we are because we are in Christ.

Standing in awe of God leads to wonder and expectation as we watch Him work in our lives and our world. It increases our desire to know Him through His Word and prayer.

One who understands his or her significance in Christ will pray more, believe more, expect more, and attempt more! If we don't derive our self-worth from Christ, then we will not attempt what He is calling us to fulfill for His glory.

My husband and I recently spent time in England for his sabbatical. We attended classes with his alma mater, Southwestern Baptist Theological Seminary, in Oxford. On one of the days, we traveled by bus to William Carey's church and the place from which God called him to missions. Many would call William Carey the father of the modern missions movement. One of the statements Carey is most famous for is emblazoned across the top of a mural at his church, "Expect great things from God; attempt great things for God."

My life's verse is Ephesians 3:20 from The Voice translation: "Now to the God who can do so many *awe-inspiring things, immeasurable things,* things greater than we ever could ask or imagine through the power at work in us." This doxology of praise acknowledges the enormity of the power at work within us.

Are you a believer that this same power works within you? It is time we live like we believe it. It doesn't matter what God is asking you to do; just say yes and step out in His power to do it. When you are not able, He is able. When you acknowledge that you can do nothing apart from Him (John 15:5), He gets all the credit. When you understand there is no way you could accomplish this, God is the one at work. All He wants is a vessel emptied of self that He can flow through and do what only He can do.

I heard a Christian speaker say once, "We will not live bolder than we believe." If my significance is not based upon my relationship with Christ, then I am basing it on myself. Self is a really small box; when we are focused on self we are so much more likely to be timid, self-absorbed, and easily offended. Once offended, we hang onto the offense and look inward, and then we become smaller and smaller. Instead of looking down and in, we are to look up and out.

When we find our significance "in Christ," we love like He loves, and we will not be easily offended. We won't "take into account a wrong suffered" (1 Corinthians 13:5). If I do not love others, then I have gotten away from His great love for me. When His love flows through me, I am significant and will be able to encourage others to find their significance in Christ.

You will sense the transformation. The people who once got on your nerves won't bother you as they once did. You will begin to see their wounds, and you will see them as God designed them. You will come alongside them and exhort or encourage them to become who He created them to be.

You will be amazed at how strong your desire will be for them to not miss what Christ has for them. You will be cheering them on as they take steps toward Christ. Because we are connected in the body of Christ we need each other. We are to "rejoice with those who rejoice, and weep with those who weep" (Romans 12:15).

All we need to be esteemed by God is to surrender to His unconditional, everlasting love. All of us have struggled with significance. As the Lord opens our eyes and makes the path light, may we take the lies captive so we can press on in the truth.

This is a challenge to all mothers and grandmothers—to women everywhere. We cannot lead our children or those we disciple where we have not been. We cannot expect them to be confident and trust the Lord with their lives if we are anxious, emotion-led women who are dependent upon others for approval and significance. We must lead the next generation in a God-confident movement to take God at His Word. Speak it. Stand on it. Live it. With great purpose and significance we must fulfill His mission.

Wisdom's Call

On what have you been depending for significance?

How will you die to your flesh and the lies of the evil one? Exchange the lie for the truth of God's Word. Choose to believe and act on God's Word. It is the truth you believe that will change the way you think and act. Write out your action plan and the truth you will stand upon:

Share with your small group the truth you are using to combat the lie. Choose to be accountable to your group and share with the members how you are taking your thoughts captive and standing on the truth.

The ways of right-living people glow with light;
    the longer they live, the brighter they shine.
But the road of wrongdoing gets darker and darker—
    travelers can't see a thing; they fall flat on their faces.

                     —Proverbs 4:18-19 MSG

Bethany's Insights

Every woman struggles with feeling insignificant at some point in her life. Recently, I went through a time of feeling insignificant, and I just couldn't shake it. I was feasting on the fiery darts of the enemy—I was overthinking his accusations. Satan was shouting at me. I was hearing that I was insignificant at my job, in my family, among my friends, and so on. I believed that everyone else was doing a better job than I was. I felt like I wasn't as qualified as others to get a certain job done. I had never really dealt with insecurity and such an insatiable longing for significance before. I wasn't focusing on the Lord and on Scripture. I was not believing who Christ has told me I am, that I am significant and seated in heavenly places in Christ (Ephesians 2:6). Instead of believing that I was robed in righteousness, I felt I was covered in shame.

Do you know what my problem was? I was staring at my own limitations instead of gazing on Christ's inestimable power (Ephesians 2:8b). The glaring issue was that I was focused on myself. I was reading my Bible and praying, but I was feasting on thoughts about me instead of shifting my thoughts to holier things. As I was talking this out with my mom, she gave me the greatest advice. She told me, "Don't live under Satan's accusations, live above the accuser!"

God has given all of us significance, not because of who we are but because of whose we are and where we are seated (Ephesians 2:6). God has provided you with your own set of gifts and capabilities to accomplish whatever He has for you. Isn't that what we are looking for in our search for significance? Don't we all want to be used by God in a special way?

Whatever God has called you to do, whether it's taking the gospel to unreached people groups across the world, to inner cities right here in America, or to your coworkers, do it knowing that your significance lies in Christ!

During my first semester of college, I was inspired by a quote I saw on Pinterest. The quote was from an elderly woman who wanted to arrive at heaven's gates having helped her neighbors tend to their gardens, having made PB&Js for kids, having taken care of the sick, and so on. That is simply not as far as I would like to take it. In response to that quote, I wrote this:

I don't want to drive up to the gates of Heaven in my nice Suburban with heated seats, DVD players, and XM radio, with my perfect little girls sitting in the latest trendy clothes and hair bows, my stout little boys wearing the best athletic gear and being the star on every sports team, my husband, the CEO of his business, wearing the most expensive suit, and I myself wearing expensive jewelry and being able to host the best party in my huge house, all while still attending church on Sunday. All of this, only to have it burned up by the fire from His eyes and being led to my new home with no treasures stored up, no feeling of relief or rest because I had been resting my way through life on Earth. I want to *run* to the gates like John the Baptist, Paul, Amy Carmichael and Mother Teresa, having been proclaiming, "prepare ye the way of the Lord!" my entire life. I desire for all of myself to be drained, used for His glory, worn out, all in, only to collapse into my Father's arms, exuberant from a race well run to receive my new body with all of my blessings stored up in Heaven! There with my Savior I will rest and reign forevermore in my *real* home.

This is the path to significance!

CHAPTER 8

PROVISION

Pay tribute to the Eternal in all of your affairs.
  Honor Him with the best of what you make.
That way you will prosper to the fullest
  and have plenty of food to eat and wine to drink.

—Proverbs 3:9-10 The Voice

God gives us principles (promises) in His Word that have very real consequences. This passage in Proverbs 3 tells us we are to honor the Lord with the best of what we make, the first of our produce. If we honor Him in this way, He will cause us to prosper and have what we need. This blessing has a prerequisite. We know this passage is making reference to the tithe, established in the Old Testament.

Malachi the prophet told the people they were stealing from God because they were not tithing. Haggai said God was poking holes in their purses (Haggai 1:6; Malachi 3:8-10). Whether or not we honor God with our tithe reveals our heart. Jesus taught that "where your treasure is, there your heart will be also" (Matthew 6:21). Are you treasuring riches or Christ?

Some argue that tithing is an Old Testament concept. But Jesus taught very clearly that He did not come to negate or do away with the law but to fulfill it (Matthew 5:17). Jesus didn't just obey the law, He superseded the law. Jesus didn't stop with saying not to commit adultery. He went on to say don't have lustful thoughts in your heart because if you do, you have committed adultery in your heart (Matthew 5:27-30).

In Matthew 23, Jesus spoke to the religious leaders of His day: "Woe to you, scribes and Pharisees, hypocrites! For you tithe mint and dill and cumin, and have neglected the weightier provisions of the law: justice and mercy and faithfulness; but these are the things you should have done without neglecting the others" (v. 23).

In that verse, Jesus affirmed tithing. But the outward act of tithing is to be the result of inward devotion to the Lord. As we "honor" Him with the tithe, we should also honor others with "justice, mercy and faithfulness." Jesus called out the weightier provisions of the law. He always went straight to the heart of the matter. God doesn't look at the outward appearance; He is looking at the heart. In the heart resides the sin that comes out through our mouths and our actions (Matthew 12:34).

One of the most beautiful pictures in Scripture of God's provision is the Old Testament account of God providing for Elijah (1 Kings 17:1-6). Elijah had just predicted there would be a drought in the land of Israel. After that pronouncement to King Ahab, God directed Elijah to go to the brook Cherith, where He had the ravens provide food for him morning and evening. As the drought affected the land, the brook began to dry up. I have always thought it was interesting that God did not have Elijah go to a new place of provision until the brook had completely dried up.

Don't you think Elijah wondered, as the brook became a trickle, just how God might provide? Do you think he worried? There is no indication that he did. When that resource was gone, God directed Elijah to the next God-appointed place of provision—a widow. And not just any widow, a Gentile widow. This God-fearing woman was preparing to make the last meal for herself and her son. But God stepped in and provided at just the right time for the widow and for Elijah.

God blessed her bowl of flour and her jar of oil, and they did not run out until the drought was over. This was truly an act of faith on her part. She used all that she had left to make bread for Elijah before making anything for herself or her son.

In his commentary, Matthew Henry stated,

> Those that deal with God must deal upon trust; seek first his kingdom, and then other things shall be added. By the law, the first-fruits were God's, the tithe was taken out first, and the heave-offering of their dough was first offered (Numbers 15:20, 21). But surely the increase of this widow's faith, to such a degree as to enable her

thus to deny herself and to depend upon the divine promise, was as great a miracle in the kingdom of grace as the increase of her oil was in the kingdom of providence. Happy are those who can thus, against hope, believe and obey in hope.[1]

God is able to supernaturally provide through natural means. The brook provided water, and the ravens provided meat and bread. Then God used an inexhaustible bowl of flour and oil. God is our Source and Provider.

The other things we so often depend on: jobs, bank accounts, education, and stock market investments are resources. These resources may run out, but our "Source" never does.

Jesus taught that God was very practical in His provision for our daily needs. He provides us with food and clothing. He is the perfect Father, and He has told His children, "So do not consume yourselves with questions: What will we eat? What will we drink? What will we wear? Outsiders make themselves frantic over such questions; *they don't realize that* your heavenly Father knows exactly what you need. Seek first the kingdom of God and His righteousness, and then all these things will be given to you *too*" (Matthew 6:31-33 The Voice).

This promise is for believers. If we will seek first His kingdom, just as the widow did, then He will provide all of our needs. These are the things we are not to concern ourselves with. We are to be focused on the weightier matters of the Kingdom.

Paul later wrote to the Corinthians,

Now this I say, he who sows sparingly will also reap sparingly, and he who sows bountifully will also reap bountifully. Each one must do just as he has purposed in his heart, not grudgingly or under compulsion, for God loves a cheerful giver. And God is able to make all grace abound to you, so that always having all sufficiency in everything, you may have an abundance for every good deed. (2 Corinthians 9:6-8)

Did you notice all of the superlatives in these verses? Look at verse 8: "And God is able to make *all* grace abound to you, so that *always* having *all* sufficiency in *everything*, you may have an abundance for *every* good deed" (emphasis added).

We are merely channels through which God's provision flows. Are you tithing to your local church? Are you praying about other ministries or individuals that God would have you support? Do you listen to the voice of the Holy Spirit when He prompts you to meet a need or to be a blessing?

Obeying God leads to great joy. My husband, Steve, and I went out to eat lunch recently after church. We always ask the server how we might pray for him or her. Our waitress said she had a praise to share with us. She said two weeks earlier another couple had asked how they might pray for her. She had hesitated to let them know that she had financial needs. But she decided to be honest and present her request. They prayed for her.

That very morning, two weeks later, she had gotten to work and found out she had received a raise and a promotion, and she was now receiving benefits. We rejoiced with her and prayed, thanking the Lord for answering her prayer and for His abundant provision.

Right after this encounter Steve noticed a young family with three small children. He felt prompted to pay for their meal. He shared with me his desire, and of course I was delighted. We asked their server for their ticket, and he laid it on our table. When our server walked up and saw the ticket, she said, "You don't need that ticket, your meal has already been paid for."

We laughed and told her that the ticket wasn't ours but another family's. She thought it was quite amusing that God was blessing us in return. She walked back by our table and said, "Someone else asked to pay for your meal, and I told them it had already been paid for. So they bought you both a piece of pie."

About that time a family stopped at our table. They had been in our worship service and were thanking my husband for his message. We asked them where they lived, and they told us Oklahoma. They were in Memphis for their son to go to St. Jude Children's Research Hospital for cancer treatment. We immediately scooted over and asked them to join us in the booth. We heard their story and were able to pray with them for their son's healing.

Needless to say, we left the restaurant that day full of joy and gratitude for God's abundant provision and for allowing us to intersect with so many people whose lives He was impacting.

God is our provider. He has provided Jesus as the substitute to die in our place that we might live, really live. If He would provide us with Jesus Christ, is there anything that He would withhold from us that we truly need? Philippians 4:19 states, "And my God will supply all your needs according to His riches in glory in Christ Jesus."

He does not want you to hoard or cling to the things of this world, but to hold them with an open hand. He doesn't bless us just for us to be blessed but so that we will be a blessing. Be a channel through which He can flow and watch as He will "make *all* grace abound to you, so that *always* having *all* sufficiency in *everything*, you may have an abundance for *every* good deed" (2 Corinthians 9:8, emphasis added).

Obey God in the area of your finances and material possessions. It is in Christ that God provides us with all that we need for "life and godliness" (2 Peter 1:3). Submit your resources to Him and look to Jesus as your ultimate Source. He will not fail you.

Wisdom's Call

Are you currently tithing to your local church?

Do you give above the tithe to support missions and ministries? What ministries do you support?

Ask the Lord to make you aware of those around you who have needs. Obey the prompting of His Spirit to meet a need for someone this week. Here are some suggestions:

- Sponsor a child through Compassion International (for more information, visit compassion.com).

- Contact your local school district and ask about their needs.

- Buy a grocery gift card and give it to a single mom.

- Take flowers to a homebound person.

- Take lunch to someone in the hospital.

- Clean the home or yard of a widow with your small group.

- Pay for the meal for the person behind you in a drive-through line.

Lindsey's Insights

I remember my first impactful lesson about God's provision and blessing in my life. I was in elementary school and had gotten thirty dollars from my grandmother for getting good grades on my report card. I already knew what I would purchase with my well-earned money, and I couldn't wait to go shopping!

Soon after receiving my reward, I attended a church service, and my heart was pricked as I heard about a special love offering we would be taking up that night. Even as a child I felt the Holy Spirit tell me to give my thirty dollars to the love offering. I was torn because I really wanted to use it for myself. But I talked with my parents after the service and decided I would give my money to the love offering instead.

A few weeks later, after my mother shared my story with the women's Bible study she led, I received an anonymous letter in the mail with thirty dollars inside! God was teaching me at a young age the importance of obeying His Spirit's promptings and watching as He poured out His blessings in return.

Now that I am older, and a mother myself, I could list countless times in my life when God provided for my specific needs in powerful and practical ways. My mom uses the illustration of holding everything we have with open palms. The Lord gives, and the Lord can take away. It all belongs to Him! With this perspective, I am able to truly live life "anxious for nothing" (Philippians 4:6).

When He prompts me to give, I know it is more blessed to obey. As my husband and I practice tithing and giving to our local church, as well as other ministries God places on our hearts, I fully trust that He will be faithful to provide all of our needs. Ultimately, the greatest provision has already been made in Christ's death and resurrection. That is truly all we really need, and it cannot be taken away from us if we belong to Him.

I have made the habit of writing in a journal each time the Lord meets specific needs in my life, answers prayers, and pours out His blessings in ways I haven't even thought to ask! As my children grow I will encourage them to do the same and will share some of the things written down in my own journals. Just as the Israelites were encouraged to pause and remember all that God had done for them and their ancestors, I want to be faithful to do the same for my own family. As we are faithful to obey, faithful to trust, faithful to remember, and faithful to pass it on to future generations, God receives the glory.

As my four-year-old quoted recently, "The Lord is my Shepherd. I have everything I need" (Psalm 23:1 ICB). May we walk closely with our true Shepherd, ready to obey, fully trusting Him for our provision.

CHAPTER 9

STRENGTH OF SOUL

And they will be life to your soul
    and fine jewelry around your neck.

—Proverbs 3:22 The Voice

My son, give attention to my words;
Incline your ear to my sayings.
Do not let them depart from your sight;
Keep them in the midst of your heart.
For they are life to those who find them
And health to all their body.

—Proverbs 4:20-22

God's Word grants life and strength to our souls. Strength of soul is literally the strength in the inner man. Paul prayed for the Ephesians "that [God] would grant you, according to the riches of His glory, to be strengthened with power through His Spirit in the inner man" (Ephesians 3:16). This strength of soul stands up in the face of trials and temptations. Strength through the power of the Holy Spirit chooses obedience.

This strength is manifest in the believer who chooses to crucify the flesh so that resurrection life might be experienced (Galatians 2:20). We will not be able to tap into this power until we choose to die to our desires, rights, and reasonings. In this death to the flesh, the Spirit is manifest and begins to live through us.

The Preacher's Commentary says, "Such trust in God leads to well-being in the very depths of our persons (v. 8). 'Bones' and 'flesh' are descriptors not just of the structure and tissue of our bodies but of our whole selves, body-spirit, tangible-intangible. This reward outstrips the promises of wealth and abundance (v. 10), as valued as those material blessings are"[1] (see also Proverbs 3:1-12).

Folly is a weak-willed woman who is easily led astray. She is dependent upon the strength of her own will and doesn't realize that she is incapable of standing against the very real schemes of the evil one and her own flesh. She will inadvertently turn against herself as she listens to her own wicked heart. She will self-destruct on the path that leads to death.

How do you strengthen your soul? You must first guard your heart:

"*Above all else*, watch over your heart; diligently guard it / because from a sincere and pure heart come the good and noble things of life" (Proverbs 4:23 The Voice).

Jesus said, "The good man out of the good treasure of his heart brings forth what is good; and the evil man out of the evil treasure brings forth what is evil; for his mouth speaks from that which fills his heart" (Luke 6:45).

The way to guard your heart is to guard your thoughts: "Finally, brothers and sisters, fill your minds with *beauty and* truth. Meditate on whatever is honorable, whatever is right, whatever is pure, whatever is lovely, whatever is good, whatever is virtuous and praiseworthy" (Philippians 4:8 The Voice). We know that meditating on what is good means that we will meditate upon God's Word.

Our souls are strengthened through the renewing of our minds (see Romans 12:2). When we meditate upon and believe God's Word, we act on His truth, since we all act out of what we believe. Believing and acting on God's Word strengthens our souls and leads to great triumphs in prayer and life.

In the Old Testament there are many examples or pictures of God working through His people when they believed and acted upon His Word. Spiritual truths lace the Word of God as redemptive threads are woven into the beautiful tapestry of God's grand redemption story. We are strengthened as we see God's hand working throughout history. I often say that biblical literacy is the greatest apologetic.

One of the supreme examples of strength of soul is recorded for us in the Book of Nehemiah. Nehemiah was used by God to rebuild the wall around Jerusalem during Judah's return from captivity.

God had first sent Zerubbabel to rebuild the temple so God could once again dwell among His people (Ezra 3–6). God used Ezra to return God's Word to its place of prominence and His people to obedience (Ezra

7–10; Nehemiah 8). Then God sent Nehemiah to rebuild the wall of protection around Jerusalem (Nehemiah 2–6).

Several years ago, my husband preached a series of sermons on Ezra and Nehemiah. One of the truths he discovered was that there was a certain order to God's command to rebuild. The temple was rebuilt first (for worship). Then the Word was honored and obeyed, and God miraculously rebuilt the wall of protection around the city.

I believe God's pattern still holds true today—worship, the Word, and then the wall. If we want to experience God's supernatural protection, we must make sure we are worshiping God and honoring His Word. Then God will build His wall of protection around us.

Nehemiah met resistance from his enemies who tried to ridicule, intimidate, and bully him to stop the rebuilding. The enemy's tactics have not changed: he tries to do the same thing to us when we are obeying God and advancing His kingdom.

We can learn much about strength of soul from Nehemiah. God had given him a job to do, and he would not come down until the job was completed (Nehemiah 6:3). When Nehemiah met resistance, he turned to the Lord in prayer. Nehemiah instilled courage in his fellow Jews by his belief in God. We would do well to learn from him and to heed his marching orders:

> When I saw their *fear*, I rose and spoke to the nobles, the officials and the rest of the people: "Do not be afraid of them; remember the Lord who is great and awesome, and fight for your brothers, your sons, your daughters, your wives and your houses." ... Those who were rebuilding the wall and those who carried burdens took their load with one hand doing the work and the other holding a weapon. As for the builders, each wore his sword girded at his side as he built, while the trumpeter stood near me. I said to the nobles, the officials and the rest of the people, "The work is great and

extensive, and we are separated on the wall far from one another. At whatever place you hear the sound of the trumpet, rally to us there. *Our God will fight for us.*" (Nehemiah 4:14-20, emphasis added)

When your family is under attack, send out a rallying cry! Like Nehemiah, we are to stand in the gap to keep out the enemy and to thwart his schemes. The enemy isolates and intimidates. Do not let him shame you into keeping silent when you are facing a battle for your marriage, your child, or your own personal walk with Christ.

God created us for relationship and to function as His body in this world. When one part of the body is hurting, the entire body is affected. When you are struggling, share your burden with a few trusted individuals who you know will pray and give you godly counsel. Then stand firm on God's character and His Word and refuse to despair.

We know the enemy schemes against us (Ephesians 6:10-12). But God has given us everything we need to stand firm against those schemes and to defeat him by the Word of God, our sword of the Spirit (Ephesians 6:17).

In fact, you have armor of faith that enables you to be victorious.

Therefore, put on every piece of God's armor so you will be able to resist the enemy in the time of evil. Then after the battle you will still be standing firm. Stand your ground, putting on the belt of truth and the body armor of God's righteousness. For shoes, put on the peace that comes from the Good News so that you will be fully prepared. In addition to all of these, hold up the shield of faith to stop the fiery arrows of the devil. Put on salvation as your helmet, and take the sword of the Spirit, which is the word of God. (Ephesians 6:13-17 NLT)

As we stand upon God's Word and align our lives with it, we are establishing Him as our Stronghold. The Bible says,

The LORD is my rock and my fortress and my deliverer,
My God, my rock, in whom I take refuge;
My shield and the horn of my salvation, my *stronghold*.

(Psalm 18:2, emphasis added)

He is the great "I Am" for your every need. Why would you ever try to stand on your own?

We are no match for the enemy. But when we depend upon the Lord, He strengthens us in our inner person through His Spirit and His Word. As He lives through us, He lifts us above our circumstances and we can then confess with the psalmist, "He only is my rock and my salvation, / My *stronghold*; I shall not be greatly shaken" (Psalm 62:2, emphasis added).

Wisdom's Call

We should study God's Word to know Him! When we approach our time in the Word as an opportunity to commune with the Father we will find ourselves growing in grace and in the knowledge of Him. We will obtain His wisdom, counsel, and divine direction for living. The wise woman will lay hold of God's sound wisdom and discretion and "they will be life to [her] soul and adornment to [her] neck" (Proverbs 3:22). Life to her soul speaks to the benefits of her private communion with the Lord, but her public life will also benefit. Her godliness will be seen as an "adornment to [her] neck" (Proverbs 3:22). This speaks of her public testimony as a woman who loves and fears God. Everyone in her sphere of influence will be aware of her strength of soul. Read Proverbs 4:20-27. Wisdom is speaking. What instruction is she giving to us?

STRENGTH OF SOUL

The foolish woman rejects God's wisdom and scoffs at God's Word. Her end is death. Learn from her. Dear friend, seek the wisdom of the Lord as a diligent Bible student. What does Proverbs 1:20 tell us about wisdom?

Wisdom is not hidden from you. She is not relegated to the seminary graduate or pastor alone. She is readily available to all who will seek after her. She pleads,

> Turn to my reproof,
> Behold, I will pour out my spirit on you;
> I will make my words known to you.

> —Proverbs 1:23

113

Bethany's Insights

Here I go … the first day at my brand new school. I'm new to this private school thing. I'm an awkward seventh grader with braces and a school uniform. To top it all off, my parents are walking me to my first class, and we are late. That I am fearful would be an understatement. I'm in a new state, new city, and brand-new school. I do not know anyone, and on the inside I am just thinking that I want to go *home*. Home is comfortable, and change is hard. Change oftentimes brings feelings of fear and anxiety. Change is always the more difficult option. However, I trusted my earthly dad and my heavenly Father that Memphis was where He wanted us; and eleven years later, I can tell you that everything turned out just fine.

I know that if I sit down with any girl in the world, she can tell me about a time in her life that made her feel out of control and caused her to fear. This is completely normal. When we look in the Bible, we see many people who were faced with scary situations. Esther is a woman whom I admire because of the way she handled herself during a very frightening time in the history of the Jews. Esther had two choices: she could strengthen her soul by trusting God and acting boldly to do what the Lord told her to do, or she could succumb to fear and miss out on being used by God in a mighty way that would change the course of history.

When I look around at the women of our day, I am hard-pressed to find very many Esthers who truly possess strength of soul. When I look around at our culture, I see women walking in fear and anxiety, worrying about *everything*. Our anxiety is out of control, and women are twice as likely to be affected as men.[2] Can we please shake our bad reputation as women and learn how to trust God, take Him at His word, and walk in boldness? How will we be world changers if we constantly walk in fear instead of strength of soul? It is easy to read about Esther and other women from the Bible who possessed inner strength, but how can I develop strength of soul as well?

First, we see that like Esther, we must seek God's counsel before human counsel. Before Esther would meet with the king, she told Mordecai to gather all of the Jews to fast while she fasted as well (Esther 4:16). Before we go out into our day, whether that is school or work or elsewhere, we must meet with the Lord to get our marching orders. The reason that so many of us walk in fear instead of strength of soul is because we have not met with the Lord to get our instructions for the day!

Second, we must become like Esther in that we would rather obey the Lord than live. Esther knew that the Lord had placed her in this kingdom "for such a time as this" (4:14), and she said, "If I perish, I perish" (v. 16). When God told Esther to move, she was no longer afraid of the king taking her life. Esther was not afraid of what humans could do to her because her identity was so wrapped up in the Lord. Even though she could have been killed, she found her confidence in God and walked boldly before the king to make her request. When Henrietta Mears discussed Esther's confidence, she said, "Those who walk in holy sincerity with Christ may walk in holy security among humanity."[3] Do we walk in the same kind of boldness as Esther did? Do we spend enough time with the Lord to let Him press upon our hearts what He has us in our position to do? He has put each one of us in the exact school, sport, club, job, and friend group we are in for a specific purpose. Oh that we may spend so much time with God that we are unimpressed and therefore unafraid of men! Then we can go forth boldly, with strength of soul, to accomplish God's plan.

CHAPTER 10
Courage

Your mind *will be* clear, *free from fear;*
  when you lie down to rest, *you will* be refreshed by *sweet sleep.*
Stay calm; *there is no need to be afraid of a sudden disaster*
  or to worry when calamity strikes the wicked,
For the Eternal is always there to protect you.
  He will safeguard your each and every step.

—Proverbs 3:24-26 The Voice

The wicked run away even when no one is chasing them;
  the right-living, however, stand *their ground as boldly as lions.*

—Proverbs 28:1 The Voice

We have read in Proverbs that the "fear of the LORD is the beginning of wisdom" (Proverbs 9:10). So you may be asking, how does fear of God differ from fear of others or of events outside our control? Fearing God is a reverential submission and respect that leads to obedience. When we fear Him, we will not fear others or our circumstances. As we walk in obedience to God and His Word, He fills us with power and right thinking.

The fear to which Folly will lead you causes you to become worried and anxious and to toss and turn at night. What causes you to worry or makes you anxious? How do you respond to the news that Iran may be creating nuclear weapons? Or is it the advances of ISIS in a world that is growing increasingly intolerant of Christianity that causes your stomach to knot up? Maybe you fear a devastating health crisis or the dissolution of your marriage. Do you fear for your children's safety or their spiritual well-being in a world that seems to have lost its way?

Television news programs sensationalize news stories and feed the fear that has immobilized so many. Whether there are riots and protests in our cities or drive-by shootings and drug deals gone bad, we can't seem to escape the ever-increasing sense of evil spreading throughout our world. Not to mention our personal internal struggles such as fear of rejection, fear of travel, fear of heights, or fear of speaking in front of groups. How are we to navigate the bombardment of negative media and fear-mongering oppression?

John tells us in 1 John 4, if we really understand the love of God, then we won't allow fear to reign in our hearts. "Such love has no fear, because perfect love expels all fear. If we are afraid, it is for fear of punishment, and this shows that we have not fully experienced his perfect love" (v. 18 NLT). Literally, we are not "mature" in love, which allows fear to choke out the life and power of Christ in our lives.

What are we to do? How do we conquer fear? Second Timothy 1:7 in the New Living Translation says, "For God has not given us a spirit of fear and timidity, but of power, love, and self-discipline [sound mind]." If God has not given it to us, who has? If we are allowing fear to control us and hold us captive, then we have given in to the spirit of the evil one.

Recognizing its origin enables us to refuse fear and the thoughts that incite it. We must not allow fearful thoughts to enter our minds. The Bible tells us we are to be "of sober spirit, be on the alert. Your adversary, the devil, prowls around like a roaring lion, seeking someone to devour" (1 Peter 5:8). *Fear devours our peace and drains us of power.*

Second Timothy 1:7 is the verse that enabled me to conquer the fear of speaking in front of groups of adults. It was an irrational fear, but one that nevertheless held me captive and caused near panic attacks. As I memorized and meditated on this verse, I asked the Lord how I could apply it to my life.

Think with me about the tools God has given us to combat fear: power, love, and a sound mind. Let's begin with power. God has given us the power to recognize the lie that incites fear. We must remember that feelings are not truth. As we are "taking every thought captive to the obedience of Christ" (2 Corinthians 10:5), we are reigning in our emotions through the power of the Holy Spirit.

As I surrender to the great love of the Lord, I am able to resist the evil one (James 4:7; 1 John 4:18). Now I am able to experience the soundness of mind that enables me to replace the lie with the truth. I have done away with the irrational thoughts of sin and replaced them with the sanity of God's Word.

As our focal passage stated: "Your *mind* will be *clear*, free from fear; /

when you lie down *to rest,* you will *be refreshed by* sweet sleep" (Proverbs 3:24 The Voice). Would you characterize your sleep last night as sweet? If not, why not? We are to stay calm with the assurance that, "the Eternal is always there to protect you. He will safeguard your each and every step" (Proverbs 3:26).

The word *courage* comes from the Latin root *cor,* which means "heart" and remains a common metaphor for inner strength. As we love the Lord with all of our *heart,* soul, mind and strength (Mark 12:30), this inner strength is released and becomes courage. Courage is truly the ability to act on our convictions regardless of the outcome. Thus our strength of soul becomes courage in the face of fear.

Are you living out what you profess to believe? As Lee Stewart wrote in her article "When Loss Meets Hope," "I needed my life shoved up against my theology."[1] What you really believe will be evident in your actions! Allowing fear to hold us captive is a lack of trust in God.

It is time we live as Proverbs says, "the right-living, however, stand *their ground* as boldly as lions" (Proverbs 28:1b The Voice). How bold are you about truth? Do you allow fear of rejection or inadequacy to keep you from speaking up for truth? Do you enter into discussions about culturally accepted norms that contradict the Word of God? Or do you cower like the cowardly lion in the *Wizard of Oz*?

You are not to look for a fight, but you are not to back down when you need to stand for righteousness. We must speak the truth, but we do it in love. It is not love to allow people to continue in deception and move headlong down the path that ends in destruction.

My husband and I traveled recently for him to speak at a state convention associated with our denomination. In the airport on the way back, we stopped in a men's store, and I encouraged him to try on a shirt. As I was waiting for him, I was listening to three young men discuss theology and mythology. There was one young man who claimed to be a new Christian.

He was telling the other two that theology had come out of mythology and that they were both trying to explain the origin of God.

You can imagine what I was thinking as I listened. I hesitantly said, "I hate to interrupt, but theology came first when the God of Creation revealed Himself to Abraham more than 1,500 years before the Greeks who invented the gods of mythology." The Christian young man turned to me and began to talk about Christ and the gospel. He was very animated and excited about his newfound faith.

The moment Christ was mentioned the other two young men slipped away and suddenly became very busy. When my husband approached the counter to purchase the shirt, the young man who had appeared the most resistant to a "religious" conversation had to come back and check him out. As we began to tell him where we had been and asked about his background, he disclosed that although he was not a Christian, his grandmother was.

By the time we left the store, Steve had shared his testimony with the young man as he explained the gospel. The young man gave us his card so Steve could send him a book he had written that the young man told us he would read.

There are many people who may appear to be resistant to the gospel. Their appearance may just be a cry for help and attention. Like Folly, they are crying out to those who are passing by seeking to find purpose and significance in a world that is scaring them to death.

Fear can also impact how parents discipline their children. Or should I say, don't discipline their children. Many parents are so afraid they will make their children angry or that their children won't *like* them if they apply discipline. The Bible is very straightforward about the parent who fails to discipline. That parent "hates" their child! Proverbs 13 says, "Those who spare the rod *of discipline* hate their children, / but those who are quick to correct them show true love" (v. 24 The Voice).

This type of diligence takes courage and consistency, and it is just downright hard work. But the benefits are eternal. Our youngest daughter was our strong-willed child. Or maybe it's just that she was number four and I was tired. But she seemed to try every boundary that we established.

As soon as she could walk she would climb out of her crib. I would put her back in, and before I could turn around, she was out and would almost beat me to the door. I would spank her and put her back in bed only to have her climb right back out.

One day after Bible study, I had gone to lunch with some friends. Our daughter had continued to throw her food off her tray after being told not to. She would literally look at me, pick up the food, and toss it as if to say, "What are you going to do about it?"

If you are a parent of a child older than two years, you have probably experienced one of these moments. In that moment you question everything you know about God's Word and your parenting skills. I was also embarrassed that my child would continue to defy me. I moved very quickly from courage and certainty to doubt and despair!

I took her to the bathroom to discipline her, and when I returned and plopped down dejectedly in my chair, my friend simply said, "You have to win." I said, "Please keep telling me that, because she is wearing me out!"

My friend was a little further down the road in parenting and knew from experience that consistency during toddlerhood pays off in the teenage years. I needed the encouragement and assurance that I was doing the right thing and needed to stay the course. We all need those encouragers along the way.

Now our youngest daughter is grown, has been married for two years and is teaching in an elementary school in the inner city. Her strong will was a blessing during high school. She determined to follow the Lord and did not waver during her teen years. I am convinced that molding her will into conformity to God's Word when she was young made her teen years much less rocky.

I am now watching my children parent their children through the fun yet physically challenging preschool years. I am able to encourage them as my friend encouraged me to stay faithful to God's Word and prayer as they train their children in the right way (Proverbs 22:6). It takes courage to stand for truth in parenting and every arena of life.

It also takes courage to stand up for truth in class and among your peers when you are in high school and college. It is so much easier to "go with the flow" and end up swept onto the broad path that leads to destruction. Remember, the Lord said "many" are on that path (Matthew 7:13). There will be times that it truly feels like everybody is doing it... whatever "it" is. That is exactly what the enemy wants you to believe as you blindly follow the crowd down the broad path.

However, the Lord told us there is another way. There is a narrow path that leads to life, but only a few find it (Matthew 7:14). Be brave. Stand firm. Listen to the words of the Lord to Joshua when he was chosen to lead the Israelites into the Promised Land, "Only be strong and very courageous; be careful to do according to all the law which Moses My servant commanded you; do not turn from it to the right or to the left, so that you may have success wherever you go" (Joshua 1:7).

What was Joshua's success dependent upon? Obeying the word of the Lord. We, too, must obey God's Word if we want to experience God's blessing and success. Don't fall for the lie or be deceived by thinking immediate gratification is more important than waiting on the Lord. It takes courage to trust in the Lord and obey. This courage is the manifestation of the strength of soul that emanates from the Holy Spirit filling a life that has submitted itself to the Lord.

Wisdom's Call

What do you fear? What keeps you awake at night?

The next time you are tempted to become anxious or to worry about something, recognize that no anxious thought originates with God. *Refuse* that thought immediately. Then in faith, *resist* the enemy. Finally, *replace* those thoughts with the truth of God's Word. If you struggle with fear, replace those thoughts with 2 Timothy 1:7, "For God has not given us a spirit of timidity, but of power and love and discipline."

How has fear been preventing you from living according to God's Word?

How will you change the way you think to match God's Word?

This is a great verse to memorize about waiting on the Lord:

> Since ancient times no one has heard,
>   no ear has perceived,
> no eye has seen any God besides you,
>   who acts on behalf of those who wait for him.

—Isaiah 64:4 NIV

Remember: Refuse, Resist, and Replace!

Alli's Insights

One of the most fearful nights of my life took place on February 5, 2008. On that night an EF-4 tornado ripped through my college campus, literally turning dormitories and vehicles upside down. I was a freshman that year, and my older sister was a junior at the same university. The tornado skipped over my building and hit the dorm next-door to mine as well as the bank behind us. The pressure knocked all eight of us who were huddled together in a tiny bathroom to the floor, breaking our windows and shrouding us in darkness. Once the train-like noise disappeared, there was an eerie silence.

Not long after the storm hit, a friend of ours came running to check on us. He told us the upperclassman dorms were "gone." That's when the real fear set in. My older sister lived in one of those dorms. I immediately began to panic, imagining every worst-case scenario possible. The following fifteen minutes or so that passed were grueling. I was finally able to get in touch with Lindsey and hear her voice assuring me she was OK. She and her roommates had made it safely inside their bathroom for shelter moments before the exterior wall of their living room was ripped off. They were able to crawl out and head to shelter.

Every student on campus was ordered to evacuate the heavily damaged dormitories and head to the main educational building for a head count. I remember talking to my mom on the phone as I ran, describing what I saw. "The buildings are gone! There is debris everywhere, and cars are upside down." Firefighters showed up expecting hundreds of body bags to be needed based on the vast destruction before them. From all eyewitness accounts, the damage was catastrophic. But by the grace of God, every life was spared. Many were injured, yet God put his hedge of protection around our school that night and performed a miracle.

After three weeks we were able to resume our classes and experience the rebuilding of our school. The once original, old dormitories were replaced with brand new, beautiful ones. A new coffee shop went in, new trees were planted, and our campus began to change dramatically for the better. A local church donated the use of a hotel it had acquired next-door to its building, and my roommates and I lived there during that spring semester. It was where three of us, myself included, would meet our future spouses.

To say the Lord provided above and beyond for our school and its students would be an understatement. He turned an incredibly scary, fearful night into a date on the calendar that will always remind me of His goodness and protection. God taught me that He is truly in control of all things, including the storms and the wind. I thank God for allowing me to experience such a scary event firsthand, because it changed my view of Him and the depths to which I trust Him. God is good, He is trustworthy, and He is in control. We do not need to fear!

Stay on Truth Street (the Way). Refuse the detours (shortcuts), distractions (fiery darts), and delays (confusion and despair) of the evil one.

CHAPTER 11

INTIMACY

For the devious are an abomination to the LORD;
But He is intimate with the upright.

—Proverbs 3:32

We all desire intimacy, but for most of us, maintaining intimacy is a constant struggle since we are afraid of being genuinely known by another person because of the fear of rejection. But this fear doesn't stop the longing. We long to be fully known and unconditionally loved. When we realize that in Christ we are able to fully experience being known and yet genuinely and eternally loved, it is truly liberating

Jesus had intimate friends. Peter, James, and John pressed in to know Jesus and were invited into a level of intimacy that the other nine were not privy to. Out of these three, John was so confident of Christ's love that he is the only disciple found at the foot of the cross. Ken Gire relates the importance of intimacy and its direct impact on our faithfulness:

> The disciples are a case in point.
>
> During the upheaval that led to Christ's crucifixion, the disciples *fell away from him in reverse order of their intimacy with him.* First was Judas, the one who had the least intimate relationship with Christ. After Judas's betrayal, the other disciples scattered. The three who had the most intimate relationship with Jesus were Peter, James, and John.[1]

We are not sure what happened to James. We know Peter followed at a distance to the courtyard and there denied that he knew Christ. Ken Gire goes on to say,

> It is no wonder that forty percent of the New Testament's teaching on love came from this disciple [John]. It is no wonder that to him

Jesus entrusted the care of his mother (John 19:26-27). And it is no wonder that years later Jesus entrusted to him the greatest revelation ever given a human being (Rev. 1:9-19).

John's love for Christ is what drew him close.

It is also what kept him close.

And it is what became his refuge, his strength, and his ever present help in time of trouble.[2]

God grants His secret counsel to those who have embraced His love and therefore trust Him and derive their identity and worth from Him. John described himself as "the disciple whom Jesus loved" (John 13:23 NIV). Do you know you are loved? Do you bask in the truth of His everlasting, unconditional love for you? Have you given Him your heart without compromise? Have you allowed Him to enthrall you with His love and enable you to enter into an intimacy you have never known existed? Until you surrender to His great love, you will not experience the intimacy you are longing for!

Jesus also interacted with and validated women. Some of my favorites are the three Marys of the New Testament: Mary the mother of Christ, Mary of Bethany, and Mary Magdalene. These three women were given insight and revelation that even some of Christ's disciples missed.

Mary of Bethany realized that Jesus was going to the cross. She anointed Him for burial just days before Calvary. Mary Magdalene was the first to see the resurrected Christ and was given instructions for the disciples.

But I am also drawn to the unnamed woman at the well in John 4. This woman was a Samaritan—an ethnic/religious half-breed—one who was accustomed to being looked down upon by the Jews. She came out to draw water during the heat of the day when no one else was at the well.

Jesus met her there and, looking past her sin, saw the broken woman on the inside. He saw the woman who, like many of us, was looking for love in all the wrong places. She was longing for intimacy but coming up short. She had not only experienced five failed marriages, but was even an outcast among her own people. Recognizing her need, Jesus asked her to go and get her husband. She admitted that she didn't have a husband. Jesus told her she had spoken correctly, that she had been married five times and the man she was living with at the present time was not her husband. Shocked at His insight, she believed she had met a prophet.

This woman had come to the well to draw water but had met the One who could offer her "living water" (v. 10). This was not water drawn from a well, but water that would quench the dry and thirsty caverns in her soul—water that would satisfy her longing for life and love. When she admitted that she and her people were waiting for the Messiah, Christ declared to her "I who speak to you am He" (v. 26). Convinced that Jesus was the long awaited Messiah, she ran back into the town to share the good news with the others. Her life was changed. She received another chance!

Have you met Jesus? He will not only give you another chance, He will give you new life! He offers you "living water," and He alone will quench your thirst for life, love, and purpose. Once you meet Him, you can't wait to tell others! Those around you will soon be able to say, "It is no longer because of what you said that we believe, for we have heard for ourselves and know that this One is indeed the Savior of the world" (v. 42).

Intimacy with Christ is our place of refuge, our source of strength, our very present help in time of trouble (Psalm 46:1). The foolish woman spends all her time trying to please others. She isn't sure who she truly is because she has never really sought to know. She has been so bound by fear of rejection that she has become whatever will allow her to fit in or be liked by others.

Have you ever known a woman who becomes like whoever she is dating? If her current boyfriend is a baseball player, she loves baseball. If he is a hunter, suddenly her social media is covered with pictures of her in camo.

If he is a musician, she knows about every concert and new recording artist.

Christ came to set us free from needing the affirmation and intimacy of others to validate our being. He draws us out to be who He created us to be. Brennan Manning wrote, "Living out of the false self creates a compulsive desire to present a perfect image to the public so that everybody will admire us and nobody will know us. The imposter's life becomes a perpetual roller coaster ride of elation and depression... The imposter is what he *does*... While the imposter draws his identity from past achievements and the adulation of others, the true self claims identity in its belovedness."[3]

What Folly doesn't realize is that her lack of intimacy with Christ is causing her to become dependent on others to meet that need. It sets her up to become desperate in her actions to have this need met. If her husband isn't meeting that need, she may become like the adulterous woman in Proverbs 7 and think that another man can meet her need for intimacy.

The foolish woman in Proverbs was religious. She told the young man she was trying to entice that she had paid her peace offerings (7:14). She had done her "duty" for God and was going out to live as she pleased. She then began to describe the lavish preparations she had made to ensnare him. Blinded by lust, they both were careening down the path that leads to destruction, completely unaware of their ultimate destination.

The unfortunate truth about lust is it is never satisfied. Covenant Eyes reported the results of a survey in their 2015 Pornography Statistics. According to a survey conducted by the Barna Group in the U.S. in 2014:

- The following percentages of men say they view pornography at least once a month: 18-30-year-olds, 79%; 31-49-year-olds, 67%; 50-68-year-olds, 49%

- The following percentages of men say they view pornography at least several times a week: 18-30-year-olds, 63%; 31-49-year-olds, 38%; 50-68-year-olds, 25%;

- The following percentages of women say they view pornography at least once a month: 18-30-year-olds, 76%; 31-49-year-olds, 16%; 50-68-year-olds, 4%

- The following percentages of women say they view pornography at least several times a week: 18-30-year-olds, 21%; 31-49-year-olds, 5%; 50-68-year-olds, 0%;

- 55% of married men say they watch porn at least once a month, compared to 70% of not married men.[4]

Is there any wonder that the divorce rate has skyrocketed and sex outside of marriage is now seen as the norm? My grown children were talking about a new television show that they were interested in watching. I rarely ever watch television but sat down to watch it with them one night over sushi and fried rice. What I saw turned my stomach. We see what the American public is feeding on and wonder why so few of our leaders are role models.

As Rosaria Butterfield stated, "What good Christians don't realize is that sexual sin is not recreational sex gone overboard. Sexual sin is predatory. It won't be 'healed' by redeeming the context of the genders. Sexual sin must simply be killed. What is left of your sexuality after this annihilation is up to God. But healing, to the sexual sinner, is death: nothing more and nothing less."[5]

According to sociologist Jill Manning, the research indicates pornography consumption is associated with the following six trends, among others:

> 1. Increased marital distress, and risk of separation and divorce,

> 2. Decreased marital intimacy and sexual satisfaction,

3. Infidelity,

4. Increased appetite for more graphic types of
   pornography and sexual activity associated
   with abusive, illegal or unsafe practices,

5. Devaluation of monogamy, marriage and child
   rearing, and

6. An increasing number of people struggling
   with compulsive and addictive sexual
   behaviour.[6]

Not only does this craving for intimacy drive many to illegitimate means, but desiring affirmation from another person may lead the foolish woman to become overly dependent on a friend. When that happens she will become exclusive in this friendship and jealous of anyone else who might take away the attention of this friend. Dee Brestin in her book, *The Friendships of Women*, said, "An emotionally dependent relationship produces bondage."[7]

The incredible miracle that takes place when we surrender to Christ's unconditional love is that we are set free to love others as we have longed to be loved ourselves. Mature believers should be able to come alongside another child of God and see the best in him or her. The Holy Spirit allows us to see others as He sees them. As I have grown in my relationship with Christ, He has given me great love and respect for His children, regardless of their level of maturity.

The ability to see who God has called and created someone to be, and to come alongside the Holy Spirit and help call that person forward, is a gift given by Him. Who God has hardwired someone to be will resonate with the call. The person may even dare to believe that what you are saying, and the Spirit is confirming, may actually be possible.

As our trust in God's love grows we become more interested in other people's stories and helping them grow in their relationship with Him. Our desire will be to see them plugged into the body of Christ and utilizing their gifts for the good of the body. As they serve, they, too, will grow. This growth enables us to work *with* God instead of *for* Him. And as we develop this intimate relationship, our inner person is satisfied, and we are able to love and meet the needs of others out of the overflow (Ephesians 4:12-13).

The wise woman knows who she is in Christ. As she matures in her relationship with Christ, she becomes what Henry Cloud and John Townsend depict in their book, *Safe People*. They describe three characteristics of a safe person:

1. Draws us closer to God.

2. Draws us closer to others.

3. Helps us become the real person God created
   us to be.[8]

Safe people make you want to know Christ more intimately. When you are around them you want to be more like Jesus. They are also inclusive. Safe people are not cliquish and don't have to put others down or exclude them to feel good about themselves. Ultimately they help you become the person God created you to be—they bring out the best in you.

Would your family and friends describe you as a *safe person*? If not, in what area do you still need to mature? When your need for intimacy is met in your personal relationship with Christ, you are free to love others and point them to Christ.

Someone once said that Jesus didn't have favorites, but He did have intimates. I believe one of the reasons John was so faithful to the Lord was because he was so secure in Christ's love for him. When we believe we are loved, then we will be secure in Christ. When we live loved, it is easy to believe that God is good, and His ways are not only best but lead to wisdom and blessing.

We sometimes tease my mom about playing favorites with her grandchildren. The beauty of it is, if you ask any one of her ten grandchildren, they would all say he or she is her favorite. I believe she loves like Christ. There is room for all of us to be related intimately to Jesus and be one of His favorites. That is why we don't need to envy people who would exclude us or mistreat us.

Matthew Henry said,

> The righteous therefore have no reason to envy them, for they have his secret with them; they are his favourites; he has that communion with them which is a secret to the world and in which they have a joy that a stranger does not intermeddle with; he communicates to them the secret tokens of his love; his covenant is with them; they know his mind, and the meanings and intentions of his providence, better than others can.[9]

Wisdom's Call

How would you rate your level of intimacy with Christ?

Do you spend time in intimate communion with Jesus on a daily basis? Have you established a place and time to meet with Him? Describe your time with the Lord.

List the three characteristics of a safe person. Commit to pray about the area in which you need the most growth.

Bethany's Insights

Intimacy is defined as, "close familiarity or friendship; closeness."[10] We all long for it. We are all created to enjoy it. Women especially are wired to crave intimacy in relationships, and we look for it in our relationships with a spouse, family, and friends. Our mood can oftentimes be determined by how we feel our relationships are going. When we find ourselves in turmoil with another person, it affects us much more than it would affect two men in an argument. We think about the conflict until it drives us crazy. We long for our relationship with that person to be reconciled so we can experience intimacy in the relationship again.

Women can be known for sucking the life out of someone in a dating relationship or even in a friendship when their needs are not being met. We sometimes trudge fearfully through our relationships. We try to make sure no one gets tired of us or bails when they figure out our set of limitations and quirks. We seem to always be screaming, "Notice me! Love me! Don't leave me!" in our relationships.

But do you know who *always* has time to spend with us? His name is Jesus, and He is always longing for a deeper relationship. He created us, and He knows us better than we know ourselves. He knows our strengths, weaknesses, and little quirks that make us who we are. Even though He fully knows us (even all of the ugly parts), He still fully loves us.

Tim Keller describes being fully known, yet fully loved so eloquently in his book *The Meaning of Marriage*. He says, "To be loved but not known is comforting but superficial. To be known and not loved is our greatest fear. But to be fully known and truly loved is, well, a lot like being loved by God. It is what we need more than anything. It liberates us from pretense, humbles us out of our self-righteousness, and fortifies us for any difficulty life can throw at us."[11]

When we find intimacy with God, we find a relationship where we don't have to try so hard anymore. We don't have to scream, "Notice me!" because

He is already mindful of us and cares for us tremendously (Psalm 8:4). We don't have to say, "Want me!" because He is already alluring us into the wilderness to speak tenderly to us (Hosea 2:14). We don't have to beg, "Spend time with me!" because He is always in our midst (Zephaniah 3:17).

How do we attain an intimate relationship with God? It really is so simple. Just as with any other relationship, in order to gain intimacy we must spend time with the other person. James 4:8 says if we draw near to God, He will draw near to us. Spending time with the Lord through Bible reading and prayer will bring a deeper intimacy into our relationship with Him. The more time we spend with God, the more satisfied we will be. Our intimate relationship with the Lord will fill us up to have plenty to share with others. *Instead of sucking the life out of all of our relationships, we will be able to pour into others what the Lord has been pouring into and teaching us.*

Discipleship groups are great, practical ways to teach others what the Lord has been teaching you. During my freshman year of high school, I was so blessed to have two senior girls disciple one of my closest friends and me. When my friend and I became seniors in high school, we in turn discipled four freshman girls. We benefitted from the intimate relationship the two senior girls had with the Lord, and in turn, were encouraged to grow in intimacy with the Lord, being able to share what we had learned with younger girls.

This mentorship is a beautiful cycle that has continued in my life. But the cycle can be broken the moment someone decides not to nurture their own relationship and intimacy with Christ. Intimacy with Christ can bring a lifetime of peace in our relationships. Won't you meet with Him today?

CHAPTER 12

LOYALTY

If you don't forsake Lady Wisdom, she will protect you.
   Love her, and she will faithfully take care of you.
Gaining sound judgment is key, so first things first: go after Lady Wisdom!
   Now, whatever else you do, follow through to understanding.
Cherish her, and she will help you rise above the confusion of life—
   your possibilities will open up before you—
   embrace her, and she will raise you to a place of honor in return.

—Proverbs 4:6-8 The Voice

I remember it as if it happened yesterday. She was in the eighth grade, and I was entering the seventh. She had beautiful, long, glistening hair and I had long, curly, frizzy hair. I watched as she whisked past me in the hall, clearly confident with her entourage in tow. I wanted to go home and iron my hair—this is what we did, for all you girls who have not known life without flat irons. I thought surely if my hair only looked like hers, I could be one of her friends too.

As women, we are relational. We long for relationships and close friends. In fact, we long for a BFF. We thrive emotionally when we find a "heart" friend. I was reminded of this truth this past summer. My husband and I attended a Ravi Zacharias Apologetics Institute study. We met another couple from our hometown at dinner. As the wife and I talked, we found that we had so much in common. She would say, have you read . . . and I would say, yes, I love that author and what about . . . and her face would light up as she finished my sentence.

At the end of the week, this precious new friend gave me a book by C. S. Lewis titled, *The Four Loves*. She had this sentence marked and underlined: "Friendship, I have said, is born at the moment when one man says to another 'What! You too? I thought that no one but myself...'"[1]

Friendships like these are a gift and need to be treated with care and loyalty. These are the friends you never tire of talking to and can shop 'til you drop with them, or just work side by side on a project, laughing and talking. You can share your heart with her knowing she "gets you." You can have deep spiritual conversations and gasp at how much time has passed. You are on the same wavelength. You can finish each other's sentences.

For those of you who are married, you have already figured out that you have more words than your husband. For most men, they use most of their words at work and really aren't ready for a long conversation when they get home. Save some of those long conversations for your girlfriends. They will help meet that need, and your husband will be grateful. I tell young women all the time, one of the best things they can do for their marriage is to have a good girlfriend.

When we think about Wisdom and Folly, we know that Wisdom is a loyal friend, but Folly would be a "mean girl." Folly is the one who wants the boy you are dating or the friend you are closest to. That is because Folly finds her worth in who she is connected with in friendships or dating.

If you have a friend who is like Folly, you need to remember that you are not responsible for her happiness and cannot make her change. But you can love her even if she sees herself as your enemy. As Hayley DiMarco said in her book *Mean Girls*, "Love is about giving, not getting. Love is about caring, not being cared for. Love is about helping, not being helped. Love reaches outside itself and gives to others. Love isn't concerned with self; it is concerned with others. The love that God commands is pure, holy, and untainted by self-gratification."[2]

Remember, God loved us while we were yet sinners (Romans 5:8). We don't love because we feel like it, we love because we are commanded to love our enemies and to pray for those who persecute us (Matthew 5:44). If we act on what is true, eventually our feelings will line up with our thoughts and actions.

I would like to insert a word of advice for all of us, but especially to the young women in high school or college—*girlfriends stick together*. Boyfriends may come and go, but girlfriends can last a lifetime. Be loyal to your friends. Celebrate their joys and weep with them in their times of grief. Allow yourself to experience true "heart" friends.

It is so important to choose your friends wisely. Your best friends should be those who challenge and encourage you to become who God has created you to be. They should bring out the best in you and point you to Jesus. We need to befriend those who are lost to be able to share Christ with them, but they should not be our closest friends.

In fact, Proverbs warns about the company you keep: "A perverse man spreads strife, / And a slanderer separates intimate friends" (Proverbs 16:28). And the New Testament warns, "Do not be deceived: 'Bad company corrupts good morals'" (1 Corinthians 15:33).

Loyalty to your friends means that you will not gossip about them or say anything behind their backs that you would not say in their presence. When my girls were teenagers, I enjoyed driving our van for cheerleading trips. It is amazing what you can learn as you quietly drive and listen to them talk. All three of our girls would tell you that the only time I interrupted was when someone started talking negatively about someone who wasn't present. I would stop them and say, "Be careful what you say, and don't say anything you wouldn't say if that person was here." It didn't take many times for them to know we don't tolerate gossip.

If you are a woman whom others like to bring their gossip to, you are responsible for stopping them. You can politely say, "I don't want to listen to anything that you would not feel comfortable saying if (the person) was standing here." My husband calls gossip garbage. He says when you listen to gossip you are allowing yourself to become a garbage dump.

Moms and disciple makers, you need to lead by example. Do not allow your children to hear you talking negatively about anyone. And we all need to guard against allowing times of prayer to become "gossip" sessions. Limit the amount of information that is shared in a group and pray in generalities. Remember what the Bible says, "Above all, love each other deeply, because love covers over a multitude of sins" (1 Peter 4:8 NIV). And in Proverbs we are told, "Hatred stirs up strife, / But love covers all transgressions" (Proverbs 10:12).

God is loyal and faithfully cares for those who seek Him. God helps us to be loyal to His Word and His plan. Scripture makes it very clear that if we are loyal to Him and His Word, He will go before us and open possibilities and opportunities that we have not even begun to ask or imagine (Ephesians 3:20).

One of the most beautiful pictures of loyalty in Scripture is the one of Ruth and Naomi. In the Book of Ruth we are introduced to Elimelech and Naomi and their two sons, a Jewish family that moves to Moab because of a famine in Bethlehem. It is there that the two sons marry Moabite women. In time, Naomi's husband dies and then both of her sons do as well. Bereft of her husband and sons, she tries to convince her daughters-in-law, Orpah and Ruth, to return to their families as she returns to Bethlehem broken and empty.

Orpah returns to her family, but Ruth refuses to leave Naomi. Somehow in the context of this family, she has seen the reality of the God of the Israelites and chooses to leave her culture and gods behind for the one true God—Jehovah. In this text we encounter the beautiful words of Ruth as she commits her loyalty to Naomi and her God: "Don't ask me to leave you and turn back. Wherever you go, I will go; wherever you live, I will live. Your people will be my people, and your God will be my God. Wherever you die, I will die, and there I will be buried. May the LORD punish me severely if I allow anything but death to separate us!" (Ruth 1:16-17 NLT).

As their story unfolds we see the spectacular provision of God for those whose hearts belong wholly to Him. Ruth honors her mother-in-law and does everything she tells her to do. God goes before her and allows her to enter a relative's field where she finds food and protection. Boaz, the owner of the field and relative, is a beautiful Old Testament foreshadowing, or picture, of Christ as the Kinsman-Redeemer. He is generous, gentle, and protective.

Boaz not only provides covering and food, but also takes Ruth as his wife. God blesses them with a son who becomes the grandfather of King David. Thus Naomi is given a family, and Ruth, a Moabitess, is grafted into the very lineage of the Messiah. Oh the glories of our God and King who rescues those whose hearts are undivided in devotion to Him!

Ruth's loyalty to Naomi and to God becomes the pathway that leads to the blessing of her lineage. God has granted us His Word, which contains the commands for living that He has granted so we can experience not only human flourishing but also depth and richness in our relationships.

Several years ago, I was asked to provide a theme for our summer series for women. As I prayed about our "Girl Talk" events, I realized that G.I.R.L. could be an acronym for God's Instructions Regarding Life. Truly through His Word and the witness of the lives of those recorded in the Bible, we have everything we need to point us to the path of life. But we must choose to walk it and not just talk it.

Think about your friends. What type of woman are you drawn to? I find I am drawn to poets and giant-slayers, just as Dee Brestin, author of *The Friendships of Women*, mentioned in her book. I am drawn to women who love the Lord and live on adventure with Him. That is what Ruth and Naomi experienced, and it is also what David and Jonathan experienced.

Dee writes about the friendship of Jonathan and David. She states that Jonathan was first bonded to David when he met him holding the head of Goliath. She goes on to say,

> It helps me to understand Jonathan's bonding to David, for I, too, am drawn to those who slay giants who have defied God.... Giant slayers seem to have better spiritual vision than other Christians. Perhaps this is because obedience, which is the essence of giant slaying, breeds deeper vision. It makes sense that God would trust those who obey with more of His wisdom. Why waste it on those who aren't going to apply it[3]

151

Make sure your friends are wise women—women who trust and obey the God they profess. Read the lyrics to this verse of the old hymn *Trust and Obey*:

But we never can prove the delights of his love
Until all on the altar we lay;
For the favor he shows, for the joy he bestows,
Are for them who will trust and obey.

Are you trusting and obeying His Word? Are you a woman who is loyal to her God, her family, and her friends? A woman who understands the loyalty of God has no trouble trusting Him, which always leads to obedience.

Wisdom's Call

Would your friends consider you a loyal friend? Can they trust you to keep their concerns confidential?

Have you ever encountered a "mean girl?" What do you remember about that experience?

Have you ever been betrayed by a friend? Describe the emotions that were involved.

What kind of friends are you attracted to? Would you consider them to be mature believers with a walk of faith that you desire to emulate?

What did you learn about loyalty from Ruth's commitment to Naomi?

Lindsey's Insights

I love how beautifully the story of Ruth and Naomi illustrates the virtue of loyalty. God created us as women to connect and relate to one another heart-to-heart. I'm so thankful the Lord has blessed me with a few friends along the way who know me—warts and all—and still choose to love me and stick by me no matter what. There is no greater feeling than to be completely known and yet completely loved. True friendships can stand the test of time, distance, and life change.

One of my life's greatest blessings has been my mother's intentional choice to daily disciple, encourage, teach, guide, and train me in righteousness. The way she faithfully led three of my closest friends and me through the ups and downs of adolescence was no exception—we called ourselves the "God Walkers." My mother's faithfulness to continue meeting with us week after week is a true picture of loyalty. I know there were times when one or more of us were less than thrilled to answer spiritual questions or share personal prayer requests. We each struggled in our own ways, and other seasons were filled with joy and victory. But as we met with the God Walkers each week we were sharpened, convicted, challenged, and inspired. And my mother's investment in us did not stop there.

She took us on trips to Atlanta, Georgia, and Gatlinburg, Tennessee. She took us to hear good teaching and to Christian concerts. She led us through the Bible, inspirational books, and Scripture memorization, and she taught us to pray. When one of us was struggling, she was right there beside us. She never spoke to us in a condemning way. Instead, she was willing to meet us right where we were and purposefully speak life-giving words to us about the amazing plans God had in store if we would only surrender to Him. Her intentional investment led each of us to honor her as one of the most influential people in our lives at "Senior Night" with our church youth group.

One of the most special gifts I've ever received was a gift my mother gave the God Walkers for graduation. She took us to eat at a steak house and presented each of us with a scrapbook that contained our parents' spiritual testimonies, Scripture verses she prayed over us often, and a place for us to write our own testimonies, the testimony of our future husbands, and even of our future children. It was our "heritage book" and it was truly a love gift.

Though miles and years have separated us, that group and my mother's love for us knit our hearts together in a way that will never be broken. We've celebrated, cried, and prayed with each other through many trials and happy moments life has brought our way.

I hope to invest in my own daughters the very same way. Isn't that what it's all about? One generation proclaiming to the next the goodness and faithful love of God? And what a beautiful picture of Christ my mother was. She truly never left my side, and neither does the Lord. No matter what life may bring, our Good Shepherd will be there walking with us, holding us by the hand. He will never leave us, nor forsake us (Hebrews 13:5).

Now, years later, I want to show my daughters what loyalty really looks like. I want them to know that there is absolutely nothing they could do to escape my love or the Father's love for them. Loyalty is a choice, not a feeling. And I choose to be loyal to my children, teaching and instructing them in the ways of the Lord, being honest with them when I mess up, faithfully serving our family even when I don't feel like it, and standing for Christ even if there comes a day when we feel as though we are standing alone. How can I do any less for my sweet Savior who did so much more for me?

I also desire to be that kind of loyal friend to others. Being a loyal friend in word and deed is one of the greatest gifts we can give. In a world of competition and criticism, we are called to build one another up, stand in the gap for others in prayer, offer a helping hand or encouraging word, and make sure no sister is left behind. And heaven help us, we may reach eternity battered and bruised, but together we can gain the crown of life.

CHAPTER 13
CROWN OF BEAUTY

She will place on your head a garland of grace;
She will present you with a crown of beauty.

—Proverbs 4:9

When my girls were in middle school and high school, there was a school-sponsored pageant that was entered by a large number of girls. It was not a preliminary for another pageant, it was really just an excuse to wear a pretty dress and makeup and experience a "princess" moment. But as with all competitions, there were those who took it way too seriously! And deep down every girl secretly longed to be the one wearing the crown at the end of the evening.

All three of our girls participated in at least one of the pageants. With each one of them we spent several weeks looking for just the right dress and practicing how they would wear their hair and makeup. We made this a social event and invited their friends to practice and participate with us. We worked together on their speeches and practiced modeling and answering interview questions. By the day of the pageant, clothes and makeup were ready, and we had rehearsed their interview and speech—they were prepared.

I encouraged our girls to have fun and not to take the pageant too seriously. A judge's opinion is just that—his or her opinion. To combat the competition and feelings of insecurity that our culture seems to force upon women, I encouraged our girls to go into the school and seek out a girl who needed help with her makeup or hair and assist her. We prayed as I dropped them off at the school and asked the Lord to use them as His ambassador. We asked the Lord to guide them to the girl or girls who needed help or encouragement. The beauty of this focus is it took their thoughts off of themselves and put them on helping someone else. This outward focus generates a God-confidence that is calming and purposeful.

Our girls did well in these pageants, and I am convinced it was largely due to their willingness to not take it too seriously and to focus on helping and encouraging others. I tried to always remind them to focus on the spiritual and eternal over the physical and temporal.

All of these girls dreamed of being the one "chosen"—the one girl who would wear the crown. If we are honest, even as adults, most of us have dreamed of being lifted out of our own life and into the one of our dreams.

If we think back on our Cinderella analogy, we will notice that the enemy wants us to be imprisoned. Whether we are imprisoned by our circumstances, or the voice we hear when we look in the mirror, the enemy succeeds when we listen to him. Our Prince desires to set us free. He has rescued us from the kingdom of darkness and desires for us to enter His kingdom of glorious life and light.

The only way to live in light of eternity is to set our hearts and minds on things above, on those things that are eternal. Choose to set your mind on things above (Colossians 3:1). Take the focus off of yourself and your circumstances and begin to seek the Lord. That is exactly what Esther was called on to do for her people, the Jews, during the time of the Babylonian captivity.

Esther and her family remained in Babylon after many of the Jews had returned to Jerusalem and were rebuilding the temple and the city. An enemy of the Jews rose to power under King Artaxerxes, the king of the Persians. When Queen Vashti was deposed, there was a beauty contest of sorts, and a new queen was chosen.

Esther was chosen as the new queen. When the existence of her people was threatened, Esther had to choose to live for someone and something greater than herself. Because she honored God and her people, God honored her. She knew she must expose wicked Haman but only after seeking the Lord through three days of fasting.

Because she sought the Lord, He moved on her behalf. The king could not sleep, and he asked for the chronicles of the kings to be brought in and read to him. As the chronicles were read the king was reminded that Mordecai, Esther's uncle, had exposed a coup but had not been rewarded.

Haman had erected a gallows with the hopes of hanging Mordecai, only to have the tables turned by the Lord. Haman was hanged instead. God honored the covenant He had made with his people and protected them from extinction.

What are you living for that is beyond the physical and temporal? How are you involved in advancing the kingdom of heaven on earth? Are you fulfilling God's purposes and plan for your life? He desires to reward you on the day you stand before Him. Will your works have eternal worth? When your works are tried by fire (1 Corinthians 3:13-15), will they come out as gold, silver, and precious stones, or as hay, wood and stubble? It all depends on what you are investing in—the things of this earth or the things of heaven.

Our church has been involved in local missions in our city through a focused effort we call Bellevue Loves Memphis. Through these quarterly projects, we have entered areas of our city that we do not normally frequent to serve our fellow citizens. We have cleaned up, painted, landscaped, and served inner-city churches, schools, and individuals.

Many of our members have developed ongoing ministries from this service. We have some who serve weekly in an apartment complex ministry. Others have participated in a community garden that provides free food for our local food bank. We purchased a mobile dental clinic that has given away more than three million dollars' worth of dental care. We have teams that lead Bible studies in prisons and serve in homeless shelters.

We have a large number who tutor through a ministry that was birthed four years ago that we named ARISE2Read. ARISE2Read is a nonprofit public charity designed to recruit churches to adopt inner-city schools and to focus on third-grade literacy. Third grade is a benchmark year. In fact,

89 percent of students in poverty who did read on level by third grade graduated on time.[1] But if a child is not reading proficiently by the end of the fourth grade, two-thirds of those students will end up in jail or on welfare.[2]

This program was developed in partnership with Shelby County Schools in Memphis, Tennessee. The goal is for each second-grade child in the adopted school to be tutored one hour once a week. It is a very simple way to serve your community with very little expense. You do not have to be an educator to tutor a child. You just need to know how to read and have a heart for children.

We have had tremendous success with these students. This is our fourth year to be in our pilot elementary school. Last year the program saw a 145 percent increase in children reading on Fry Sight Word Grade Level (this is the 1,000-word list that we use in the program. There are many Internet sites that contain the list of words as well as games and activities). Their achievement test scores in reading have increased 68.75 percent in the last two years.

We also connect the church that adopts the school with a church in the community that they can come alongside to help minister in the neighborhood of the school. They work together to staff a Good News Club (a Bible club through Child Evangelism Fellowship) that meets one afternoon a week after school. You can learn more about this program which is spreading across our state and into other states by going to our website ARISE2Read.org.

I spoke recently to a group of businesspeople from across our city. I was able to stress to them that the children of our communities are our responsibility. As believers we know we are commanded by God to love our neighbor as we love ourselves. The people and families of our city are our neighbors. Do you love them as you love yourself? Are you caring for them the same way you care for yourself and for your own?

But even for those who are not believers, as community members and citizens of our cities and counties, we are responsible for our children. These children are our future and will be in leadership when we are entering our golden years. We had better lead them and love them well so they will be the educated, competent, and compassionate leaders we need for our own future.

Just as my girls found great confidence and purpose in serving other girls in the beauty pageants, we will find great joy and confidence when we serve our fellow man. It doesn't matter where the Lord takes you; serve Him. See where He is working and join Him.

Wisdom's Call

Read the story of Esther in the Old Testament. How do you think she
and the other girls felt when they were taken into the King's harem to be
possibly chosen as the next queen?

How did God give her wisdom after the three day fast that she and her
maidens and family participated in?

What did God do to elevate Mordecai?

How was Haman hanged by his own sin? Proverbs 5:22 says, "His own iniquities will capture the wicked, / And he will be held with the cords of his sin."

Alli's Insight

She will place on your head a garland of grace [God's unmerited favor]; She will present you with a crown [emblem of glory worn by the High Priest] of beauty.
——Proverbs 4:9

You know those girls who grow up never seeming to have an awkward stage? The ones all the guys want to date and all the girls want to look like? Yeah, I was not one of those girls. I've always seen myself as the "chubby middle sister" if I'm being honest. This assessment was verified after watching home videos one Christmas at my parents' house. I was a weirdo! I played Barbies with my younger sister way too long, had hair down to my belt loops, and I had a lot of black eyeliner around my pale blue eyes and equally pale skin. I wanted to wear my older sister's cute clothes, but let's face it, we were just *not* the same size. It wasn't cute.

But you know what? Even as an awkward middle schooler and early high schooler I was really happy. I loved the Lord, my church, our youth group, my friends, and even my school. Sure, I definitely had insecure times throughout, like when I was called "fat" and "piggy" in middle school or when I didn't make the cheerleading squad for my sophomore year of high school. But it wasn't until I came out of my awkward stage and entered the last two years of high school that I became very insecure and unhappy.

It wasn't until people started calling me "pretty" and "skinny" that I felt the most unattractive. It was during this time that I stopped looking to Christ for my security and worth and began looking to the world for fulfillment. You see, I thought that if I could just be in this friend group, go to these parties, or date this guy that I would feel good about myself, but it turns out the opposite occurred. The more I searched for value outside of what I knew to be true, the more lost I became.

During this dark time in my life, the Lord did not allow me to stray for long before He began pulling me back. He used countless people in my life in various ways to point me back to Truth. I thank the Lord for His continuous pursuit of me and for all of the godly people with whom He surrounded me.

I began living my life for Him going into college. It was during this time that I met my husband and got married the summer before my senior year. We graduated, moved to seminary for my husband to study to become a pastor, had our daughter, moved to Memphis for an internship, had our son, and now we live in Oklahoma. Here my husband serves as pastor at the First Baptist Church in our little town. God has proven Himself faithful time and time again.

Most importantly, He has shown me that when I look to the world for security and satisfaction I will walk away feeling defeated and unlovely. But when I look to God for these things, I am filled with the righteousness of Christ. I am a child of God, a coheir with Christ, looking forward to my heavenly inheritance in glory—and the same can be said of you! Knowing *who* we are in Christ enables us to lay aside those old insecurities and walk in freedom and confidence before the Lord.

We will never be perfect, which is why Jesus' righteousness freely given to us is such a beautiful blessing! When God looks at us, He doesn't see our sinfulness and filth, He sees his beautiful daughter whom He loves. We must walk in this new identity, looking forward to eternity with our heavenly Father!

Garlanded with grace and crowned with beauty—
you have been clothed like royalty—act like it!
Live from your belovedness and you will be changed
from the inside out—beautiful for our Heavenly Bridegroom
and prepared for the greatest celebration in the universe—
the Marriage Supper of the Lamb!

CHAPTER 14

Blessed and Happy

So now listen to me, my children:
  those who live by my ways will find true *happiness.*
Pay attention to my guidance, dare to *be wise,*
  and don't disregard my teachings.
The one who listens to me,
  who carefully seeks me in everyday things
  and delays action until my way is apparent, that one will find true
    happiness.
For when he [she] recognizes and follows me, *he [she] finds* a peaceful and
    satisfying *life*
  and receives favor from the Eternal.

—Proverbs 8:32-35 The Voice

Paul's epistle of joy, the Book of Philippians, was written from a jail cell. Paul's ability to find joy in the midst of trial is a picture of what we depicted at the beginning of the book with the story of Cinderella. Cinderella had been changed from the inside out. Because she met the prince, her world had been changed. Her circumstances no longer defined her. Cinderella's heart belonged to the prince, and she knew her destiny was with him.

Paul knew that it didn't matter where this life took him; a Philippian jail cell or Caesar's prison, God was sovereign and would be glorified in and through him if he surrendered to God's plan. Paul saw beyond this life to the real life, the one yet to come. The good life was purchased for us by Christ, who is preparing a place for us (John 14:2). He lived for a larger kingdom and a greater agenda.

The wise woman lives from a Kingdom vantage point. She has an eternal perspective. She is able to choose wisely because salvation has changed not just her destination but her destiny. "[God] has granted to us His precious and magnificent promises, so that by them you can become partakers of the divine nature, having escaped the corruption that is in the world by lust" (2 Peter 1:4). The knowledge of these promises allows us to appropriate His divine power.

The wise woman is not just a good person. She is not just a religious person who adheres strictly to a code of ethical behavior. She is not just playing church. She is not just patched up; she is pardoned! She has been set free from the bondage of sin, Satan, and self. She is a partaker of the divine nature of our Father. Filled with His Spirit, she chooses life and experiences the joy and love that comes with it!

Our ability to enter into and enjoy the abundant life is directly related to our willingness to choose to die to self so that we might come alive in Christ. Real life is the Christian life, the Spirit-filled life. This life is entered through death to the flesh. We must wage war on our sin so that we might experience the abundant life Christ died to purchase. This is not a fleshly approach that says I can live however I want to because I am under grace. It is not legalism or the opposite—a faith that glorifies or dismisses failure.

As Rosaria Butterfield said in her book, *Openness Unhindered,*

> Sin must be dealt with in a posture of Christian combat, not in expected or celebrated defeat and failure. We are to use the full armor of all of the means of grace that God gives to us. This position teaches us that conversion gives you freedom from the crime of sin and gives you liberty to respond to God's grace of conversion through repentance and obedience. Conversion gives you the freedom to repent, not the freedom to expect failure. It was then that I got it: repentance and the love for God—and the obedience to his law that grows from them—were the missing links between shame and grace.[1]

So often, we believe the lie that if we obey God, we are going to "miss out" on happiness. We fall for the deception of the evil one and our flesh, believing if we will satisfy our longings apart from God, we will find true happiness. This is exactly what Folly sought to do. She called out to people at the point of their desires and tried to entice them to find fulfillment of their needs in anything other than Christ. In reality, life apart from God, which is sin, separates us not only from God but also from all that will satisfy and bring ultimate happiness.

In a blog post for *The Gospel Coalition*, Jen Wilkin called this defeatist frame of mind "'celebratory failurism'—the idea that believers cannot obey the law and will fail at every attempt." She went on to say,

Furthermore, our failure is ultimately cause to celebrate because it makes grace all the more beautiful.

These days, obedience has gotten a bad name. And failure has gotten a make-over …

The gospel grants both *freedom from* the penalty of sin and *freedom to* begin to obey (Romans 6:16). And what are we to obey? The Law that once gave death now gives freedom.[2]

Free to obey. That is the beauty of the abundant life that Jesus Christ died to purchase for us. Obedience precedes blessing and further revelation. This revelation of Christ in and through His Word brings the joy and wonder we are longing for.

But we, like Christ, must experience death that we might walk in resurrection life and power. We must die to our flesh. To quote Rosaria again, "Because of God's righteousness, we honor his standards for holiness by vigilantly putting to death all idols and by refusing to be idol-makers, even when it means getting a different job (and one with less prestige), choosing better friends, or throwing away your smart-phone."[3]

We cannot reason with our flesh, coddle it, or control it—we must mortify it. It must be taken to the cross that we might enter into the freedom of obedience.

God the Father, through Christ, has invited us into the joy of the Lord and the very oneness of essence the Godhead enjoys (John 17:20-21). Christ prayed that we would experience being one, "just as We are one; I in them and You in Me, that they may be perfected in unity" (John 17:22-23).

Genesis through Revelation tells a story, the story of Jesus. If we go back to the very beginning, we will see in Genesis 1 that God spoke eight times in Creation, and matter responded. God the Father, Son, and Holy Spirit were present at Creation and brought all things into being.

The Bible begins with, "In the beginning God." Then it tells us in Genesis 1:2b, "the Spirit of God was moving over the surface of the waters." We know the Word through which God created was the Son, Jesus Christ (John 1:1). So we are introduced to the Trinity in the very beginning. This Godhead, three in one, experiences oneness of essence and yet are three distinct persons.

God said, "Let Us make man in Our image" (Genesis 1:26). Adam and Eve were one in marriage and in essence. They were naked and unashamed; there was no separation. Sin separates. In Genesis 3 we see how sin separated Adam and Eve from God and from each other.

This pain and relational brokenness has reverberated throughout history. You and I deal with the ramifications of the separation caused by sin—our own sin and the sin of others against us.

Christ came that He might provide *the way* back to the Father and the oneness God intended. "The Word became flesh, and dwelt among us, and we saw His glory, glory as of the only begotten from the Father, full of grace and truth" (John 1:14).

Jesus was born of a virgin and consequently without a sin nature. He was fully God and yet fully human. He lived a sinless life that He might take our place and pay the penalty for our sin, that He might do away with separation.

Jesus taught His disciples on the night before His death in John 14–16. He experienced the Passover meal with them and instituted the Lord's Supper. It was after this meal that Jesus led His disciples to the garden of Gethsemane where He would agonize over His upcoming crucifixion.

But I believe Christ agonized over so much more than the physical pain of crucifixion, as horrible as that would be. He was agonizing over the separation from God that would take place the moment He took upon Himself the sin of the world (1 Peter 2:24). Throughout all of eternity, the Godhead had enjoyed relational oneness. Upon that cross, Christ would cry out, "My God, My God, why have You forsaken Me?" (Matthew

27:46). For the first time in all of eternity, there was no response. Bearing my sin and your sin, Christ was separated and forsaken so that we might never be separated again.

Now, in Christ, we are one with the Father through the Holy Spirit. Sealed by His Spirit who was sent on the day of Pentecost, we are one when we are in Christ. We are also united as members of His body. Unity is a picture of the Godhead and that is why the enemy seeks to divide. He knows the power that is manifest when we are reconnected to God and to each other.

Peter tells us in 2 Peter 1:4 that through His precious and magnificent promises we may become "partakers of the divine nature" just as Jesus had prayed for His followers in John 17. This oneness with Christ leads to unity in the body of Christ. I believe this unity depicted by love is the sign of spiritual maturity and will lead to the greatest level of joy. As Peter said in 1 Peter 1:8, "And though you have not seen Him, you love Him, and though you do not see Him now, but believe in Him, you greatly rejoice with joy inexpressible and full of glory." This is the joy we long for and can only experience in Christ.

Matthew Henry articulated so straightforwardly, "So plainly, so pressingly, is the case laid before us, that we shall be for ever inexcusable if we perish in our folly."[4]

As we have seen in our study of Proverbs 1–9, God has made the two paths abundantly clear. The issue is not that we don't know the truth but that we have not accepted our position as beloved. Therefore, we believe what we are reading may apply to others but would not work for us.

Do you want to be happy; I mean really happy? Stop listening to the enemy. Choose Jesus. Immerse yourself in His Word and then put it into practice.

As Randy Alcorn says in his book, *Happiness*, "When we seek holiness at the expense of happiness or happiness at the expense of holiness, we lose both the joy of being holy and the happiness birthed by obedience. God commands holiness, knowing that when we follow his plan, we'll be happy."[5]

Let's review the two paths of Wisdom and Folly—and understand that both women are calling to those who are passing by going right or "straight on their way" (Proverbs 9:15 NIV). We see through God's Word a pattern, that there are:

Two trees
Two choices
Two paths
Two voices

Curses of Folly	*Blessings of Wisdom*
Insecure	Secure in Christ
Tactless	Discreet
Foolish	Understanding
Insignificant	Significant in Christ
Lust for more	Provision
Weak-willed/unstable	Strength of soul
Fearful/anxious	Courageous
Codependent/flatters/seduces	Intimacy
Disloyal/untrustworthy/lies	Loyal
Bitterness of death	Crown of beauty
Cursed	Blessed/happy
Death/Separation	**Life: Abundant and Eternal, United with Christ**

The beauty of eternity will be the glorious revelation that there is no end to "happily ever after!"

CONCLUSION

In Proverbs 31 we are introduced to the virtuous woman, the woman who is revered for her fear of God. She is not a perfect woman as some have thought; she is godly. She is not striving; she is living out of the center of a life that fears or reveres God, and her choices prove it.

God alone is our source for wisdom, strength, grace, love, and joy. The virtuous woman is simply a picture of a woman whose life reflects her relationship and commitment to God. I encourage you to allow her, this woman that God praises, to be a role model for you and your daughters or the women you disciple.

Isn't it interesting that Proverbs ends as it began, admonishing us to fear the Lord. The Bible itself ends in reverse order of its beginning. Just as the first three chapters of Genesis recount Creation (chapters 1–2) and the Fall (chapter 3), Revelation unveils the truth of God's ultimate plan for humanity. The last three chapters of the Bible undo all that the enemy had sought to undermine and destroy. Revelation 20 records the destruction of the devil, death, and the grave. Revelation 21–22 unfolds the beauty of the new creation. God destroys the curse and reverses all that the curse has affected.

And glory of glories in Revelation 22:1-4 we read that there is only "one" tree in the New Jerusalem, the tree of life! There is no more opportunity to choose sin—only life and blessing!

Oh dear friend, this is God's desire for you. He has made Himself known through your own conscience and the beauty of all He has created (Romans 1:19-20). He holds it all together and is the One who gives you breath. His plan for you is for your good to give you a future and a hope (Jeremiah 29:11). But you must choose! Choose wisely. Choose Jesus! And when you do, you will be leaving a legacy of blessing for your descendants that will impact thousands (Exodus 20:5-6). Choose Jesus, and you will be a wise woman on the path that leads to life!

APPENDIX A

Suggestions for Discipling Teens

My suggestions for meeting with teens:

1. Choose a weekly time to meet. Many youth groups have Wednesday night Bible studies or meetings. One of the times that worked best when I was meeting with my daughters and their friends was on Wednesday evenings before their Bible study. Often we met at church, but about once a month we met at a local Mexican restaurant. Allow at least an hour for discussion and prayer together. With my youngest daughter, our small group met at a local coffee shop one afternoon a week.

2. Read through the Bible annually. There are many plans that you can choose from, but the easiest is a One Year Bible in a translation that is easy to understand. I typically use the New Living Translation.

3. Memorize Scripture. The Navigators have a topical memory system that is easy to use. I like to use ring-bound 5-by-7-inch cards to write out the memory verses I assign. Have your disciples recite

their memory verses each week. This accountability helps us all accomplish these goals.

4. Pray together. Most of us learn to pray by praying with others. Write down their requests and follow up on the answers.

5. Read good Christian books. I have a suggested reading list of Christian books I recommend for my discipleship groups in Appendix C. I recommend assigning two or three chapters a week, depending on the size of the chapters.

6. Expose them to Christian speakers and recording artists. Make plans to go together to concerts and conferences.

7. Invite them into your home and your life. Many young people live in broken homes and long for a mentor to allow them to experience how Christian families function. Stock the pantry and refrigerator. Invite them over for meals or to spend the night. We had so many wonderful conversations around my kitchen table late at night.

APPENDIX B

Suggestions for Discipling Women

I currently disciple women in my home on Thursday mornings. I like hosting the group in my home because it is less sterile than a church classroom. Women seem to relax almost immediately and feel that they know me well by just being in my great room. In fact, I am sitting in that room right now. I have a chair and ottoman in the corner where I meet with the Lord each morning. I have piles of books and Bibles around me, and my computer is in my lap. This is my happy place.

My home does not have to be immaculate, and there are often weeds in my front flowerbed to greet them as they approach the front door. I offer them coffee or water and then we jump right in. This is not about me; it is about getting to know God. That should help take the pressure off of opening our homes.

We use a two-hour format, which gives us time for:

1. Scripture memory review (10 minutes);

2. Discussion of the Chronological Bible portion reading that week (we use the One Year Chronological Bible NKJV, 15-20 minutes);

3. In-depth study of the current passage
   (40 minutes);

4. Discussion of any additional book we are
   studying (20 minutes);

5. Prayer (30 minutes).

About once a month, I put on a pot of soup and invite the women to stay for lunch. We are able to have further discussion, get to know each other better, and just enjoy fellowship.

We have grown in our relationship with each other through group texts and e-mails that keep us updated on prayer requests. We have gone to Christian movies together, gone out to lunch together, and served individuals in the group when there is a need.

I keep my groups for two years and then launch them to lead groups of their own. I use *W3: Women, Worldview, and the Word* by Iva May (chrono logicalbibleteaching.com). Iva teaches a biblical worldview by breaking down the Bible into fourteen time periods or eras. She works through fifty-two main stories from Scripture that reveal God, humanity, and sin and then makes connections as threads of truth are traced throughout Scripture.

I have found that most people have very little understanding of the Old Testament. Without this foundational knowledge it is difficult to value all that Christ purchased for us through His life, death, and resurrection. It is also difficult to maintain truths that are learned without a place to "hang" them on a biblical timeline. Once this timeline is comprehended, increased understanding results in not only greater knowledge but greater application and life change.

APPENDIX C
Suggested Reading List

7 Women by Eric Metaxas

Celebration of Discipline by Richard J. Foster

Concentric Circles of Concern by W. Oscar Thompson Jr.

Connecting by Larry Crabb

Counterfeit Gods by Tim Keller

Feminine Appeal by Carolyn Mahaney

God's Story by Anne Graham Lotz

Grace Based Parenting by Dr. Tim Kimmel

Growing True Disciples by George Barna

Holy Available by Gary Thomas

Hour That Changes the World, The by Dick Eastman

Invisible War, The by Chip Ingram

Knowledge of the Holy, The by A. W. Tozer

Love and Respect by Dr. Emerson Eggerichs

Meaning of Marriage, The by Tim Keller

Mere Christianity by C. S. Lewis

One Thousand Gifts by Ann Voskamp

Out of the Salt Shaker by Rebecca Manley Pippert

Own Your Life by Sally Clarkson

Praying God's Word by Beth Moore

Praying Life, The by Jennifer Kennedy Dean

Pursuit of God, The by A. W. Tozer

Real-Life Discipleship by Jim Putman

Reason for God, The by Tim Keller

Reclaiming Surrendered Ground by Jim Logan

Release of the Spirit, The by Watchman Nee

Sacred Influence by Gary Thomas

Sacred Marriage by Gary Thomas

Safe People by Dr. Henry Cloud and Dr. John Townsend

Safest Place on Earth, The by Larry Crabb

Secret Thoughts of an Unlikely Convert, The by Rosaria Champagne
   Butterfield

Spiritual Authority by Watchman Nee

Tale of Three Kings, A by Gene Edwards

Total Truth by Nancy Pearcey

What the Bible Is All About by Henrietta Mears

What's So Amazing About Grace? by Philip Yancey

When Godly People Do Ungodly Things by Beth Moore

Windows of the Soul by Ken Gire

With Christ in the School of Prayer by Andrew Murray

Women of the Word by Jen Wilkin

Biographies

A Chance to Die: The Life and Legacy of Amy Carmichael by Elisabeth Elliott

Autobiography of George Müller, The

Autobiography of Jeanne Guyon, The

Bonhoeffer: Pastor, Martyr, Prophet, Spy by Eric Metaxas

Dream Big: The Henrietta Mears Story edited by Earl O. Roe

Go Home and Tell—Autobiography of Bertha Smith

Praying Hyde, Apostle of Prayer: The Life Story of John Hyde, edited by
Captain E. G. Carré

Reese Howells: Intercessor by Norman Grubb

Through Gates of Splendor by Elizabeth Elliott

APPENDIX D

SPIRITUAL LEGACY JOURNAL

In chapter 12, my daughter Lindsey told about a heritage or legacy journal that I gave to her and her three friends whom I had discipled throughout high school. I had contacted their parents and asked them to send me their testimonies, as well as what they remembered about when their daughter committed her life to Christ. These testimonies, Scripture, and a letter from me were included in their books.

I later made one for Alli. When Bethany was approaching graduation, her Sunday school teacher asked if she could make journals for Bethany and the girls she had discipled since they were in the seventh grade. This precious gift is like passing the baton to the next generation. This gift and challenge expresses that the disciple is now responsible for passing on what she has learned to someone else and eventually to her own family.

APPENDIX E

Prayer Notebook

A notebook is obviously not the only method that works for prayer. Many different methods have been used through the years. My husband uses blank index cards to write out his prayer requests and prays through them. I have a friend who uses a new prayer journal each year. But this simple notebook has worked for me for almost twenty years. *I encourage you to find a plan that works for you and implement it.*

Here is how my notebook is organized:

I use a simple three-ring notebook, notebook paper, page protectors, and dividers. These are the sections I use with the dividers:

- Praise—These entries are Scriptures I pray to the Lord ascribing to Him His glory. The Psalms are great to pray back to the Lord.

- Family—I use page protectors to insert pictures so I can look at their faces as I pray for them. I have a page or pages for each family member that contain requests as well as Scriptures that I pray for them.

- Church—I have a list of our staff members and specific Scriptures I pray for them and their families.

- Friends—We have many friends in ministry for whom I pray on a regular basis.

- Intercession—When someone asks me to pray for him or her, I write the name down with the specific request. I date the requests and then write down the answer later. I have lists for physical healing, couples who desire children, singles who desire marriage, my discipleship group and their families, and so on.

- Government—I pray for local, state, and national government.

- Missions and the World—I pray for missionaries and mission trips that I am taking or that church members are participating in. I also pray for mission organizations such as Compassion International and the child we sponsor. In this section, I like to include a world atlas.

You will not be able to pray through the entire notebook every day, so you will need to decide on a plan. I pray for my family every day, and then have different days that I pray for the other sections. For instance, I pray for our church staff on Wednesdays and Sundays. Work out your plan dependent upon the amount of time you have for your personal time with the Lord. Remember to allow at least fifteen minutes for Bible reading as well.

NOTES

Introduction

1. "Romance Statistics," Romance Writers of America website, www.rwa.org/p/cm/ld/fid=580.

2. Vocabulary.com, *s.v.* "enthralled," accessed June 2, 2017, www.vocabulary.com/dictionary/enthralled.

3. Gary Thomas, *Thirsting for God* (Eugene, Oregon: Harvest House, 2011), 74.

3. Choose

1. Oswald Chambers, "The Habit of Rising to the Occasion" in *My Utmost for His Highest*, updated, ed. James Reimann (Grand Rapids: Discovery House, 1991), 135.

4. Real Wisdom

1. Jonathan Akin, *Preaching Christ from Proverbs* (Nashville: Rainer Publishing, 2015), 75.

2. Randy Alcorn, *Happiness* (Carol Stream, IL: Tyndale House, 2015), xii.

3. Watchman Nee, *Spiritual Authority* (New York: Christian Fellowship, 2014), 17.

5. Security

1. Carolyn Coker Ross, MD, "Why Do Women Hate Their Bodies?" *World of Psychology* (blog), June 2, 2012, www.psychcentral.com/blog/archives/2012/06/02/why-do-women-hate-their-bodies/.

2. Ross, *World of Psychology* (blog).

3. Chera Hodges, "7 Strategies For Dealing With Insecurity," Lifescript, May 7, 2013, www.lifescript.com/well-being/articles/0/7_strategies_for _dealing_with_insecurity.aspx.

4. Renee Swope, *A Confident Heart* (Grand Rapids: Revell, 2011), 22.

5. James Stewart, *Still Waters* (Philadelphia: Revival Literature, 1962), 108.

6. Sharon Begley, "In the Age of Anxiety, are we all mentally ill?" Reuters website, July 13, 2012, www.reuters.com/article/us-usa-health-anxiety-idUSBRE 86C07820120713.

7. Brené Brown, *Daring Greatly* (New York: Avery, 2012), 153.

8. Tim Keller, "A World of Idols" (sermon) from The Church—How to Believe Despite Christians series, March 29, 1998, Acts 17:16-34, Redeemer App, podcast.

9. Jen Wilkin, *Women of the Word* (Wheaton, IL: Crossway, 2014), 26.

6. Discretion and Understanding

1. *Merriam-Webster Dictionary*, s.v. "discretion," www.merriam-webster.com /dictionary/discretion.

2. *Merriam-Webster Dictionary*, s.v. "understanding," www.merriam-webster .com/dictionary/understanding.

3. Portia Nelson, *There's a Hole in My Sidewalk: The Romance of Self-Discovery* (New York: Atria Books, 2012), xi-xii.

4. Bruce Wilkinson, *Your Daily Walk: 365 Daily Devotions to Read Through the Bible in a Year* (Wheaton, IL: Tyndale House, 1997), 225.

7. Significance

1. Larry Crabb, *The Marriage Builder* (Grand Rapids, MI: Zondervan, 2013), 35.

2. David A. Hubbard, *Proverbs*, vol. 15 of Old Testament in The Preacher's Commentary Series, ed. Lloyd J. Ogilvie (Nashville: Thomas Nelson, 1989), 72.

3. Sally Clarkson, *Own Your Life* (Carol Stream, IL: Tyndale Momentum, 2014), 71.

4. Robert S. McGee, *The Search for Significance* (Nashville: Thomas Nelson, 2003), 20.

8. Provision

1. Matthew Henry, *An Exposition of the Old and New Testament* (London: Joseph Robinson, 1839), 668.

9. Strength of Soul

1. David A. Hubbard, *Proverbs*, vol. 15 of Old Testament in The Preacher's Commentary Series, ed. Lloyd J. Ogilvie (Nashville: Thomas Nelson, 1989), 73.
2. Anxiety and Depression Association of America, "Facts," accessed February 24, 2017, www.adaa.org/living-with-anxiety/women/facts.
3. Henrietta Mears, *What the Bible Is All About* (Ventura, CA: Regal Books, 2011), 196.

10. Courage

1. Lee Stewart, "When Loss Meets Hope," February 23, 2015, Missional Motherhood website, www.missionalmotherhood.com/infertiltymiscarriage/loss-meets-hope/.

11. Intimacy

1. Ken Gire, *Life as We Would Want It . . . Life as We Are Given It: The Beauty God Brings from Life's Upheavals* (Nashville: Thomas Nelson, 2006), 53, emphasis added.
2. Gire, *Life as We Would Want It*, 54–55.
3. Brennan Manning, *Abba's Child* (Colorado Springs: NavPress, 2015), 16-17, 33.
4. Covenant Eyes, PDF, "Pornography Statistics: 250+ Facts, Quotes, and Statistics About Pornography Use" (Owosso, MI: Covenant Eyes, 2015), 8. PDF available for download at www.covenanteyes.com/resources/download-your-copy-of-the-pornography-statistics-pack.
5. Rosaria Champagne Butterfield, *The Secret Thoughts of an Unlikely Convert* (Pittsburgh: Crown & Covenant, 2012), 83.
6. Jill Manning, Testimony, "Hearing on Pornography's Impact on Marriage and the Family," November 10, 2005, U.S. Senate Hearing, Subcommittee on the Constitution, Civil Rights and Property Rights, www.judiciary.senate.gov/imo/media/doc/manning_testimony_11_10_05.pdf.

NOTES

7. Dee Brestin, *The Friendships of Women* (Colorado Springs: David C. Cook, 2008), 84.

8. Henry Cloud and John Townsend, *Safe People* (Grand Rapids: Zondervan, 1995), 143.

9. Matthew Henry, *Matthew Henry's Concise Commentary on the Whole Bible*, BibleGateway.com, www.biblegateway.com/resources/matthew-henry /Prov.3.27-Prov.3.35.

10. *English Oxford Living Dictionaries*, s.v. "intimacy," https://en.oxforddiction aries.com/definition/us/intimacy.

11. Tim Keller, *The Meaning of Marriage* (New York: Dutton, 2011), 87.

12. Loyalty

1. C. S. Lewis, *The Four Loves* (New York: Harcourt, 1971), 78.

2. Hayley DiMarco, *Mean Girls* (Grand Rapids: Revell, 2008), 49.

3. Dee Brestin, *The Friendships of Women* (Colorado Springs: David C. Cook, 2008), 147–48.

13. Crown of Beauty

1. Sarah D. Sparks, "Study: Third Grade Reading Predicts Later High School Graduation," April 8, 2011, *Education Week* website, http://blogs.edweek.org /edweek/inside-school-research/2011/04/the_disquieting_side_effect_of. html.

2. Begin to Read, "Literacy Statistics," accessed February 24, 2017, http:// begintoread.com/research/literacystatistics.html.

14. Blessed and Happy

1. Rosaria Champagne Butterfield, *Openness Unhindered* (Pittsburgh: Crown & Covenant, 2015), e-book.

2. Jen Wilkin, "Failure Is Not a Virtue," May 1, 2014, The Gospel Coalition website, www.thegospelcoalition.org/article/failure-is-not-a-virtue.

3. Butterfield, *Openness Unhindered*, e-book.

4. Matthew Henry, *Matthew Henry's Concise Commentary on the Whole Bible* (Peabody: Hendrickson, n.d.), 962.

5. Randy Alcorn, *Happiness* (Carol Stream, IL: Tyndale, 2015), xii.